DIABETIC DIET AFTER 60 FOR BEGINNERS

2000+ DAYS OF SIMPLE, QUICK, LOW-CARB, LOW-SUGAR RECIPES TO MASTER PRE-DIABETES AND TYPE 2 DIABETES, COMPLETE WITH A 30-DAY MEAL PLAN, SHOPPING LISTS & DINING OUT TIPS

William Brashear

DISCLAIMER

The information provided in this book is for general informational purposes only and should not be considered medical advice. Always consult with your healthcare provider before making any dietary or lifestyle changes. The author and publisher are not responsible for any adverse effects or consequences resulting from the use or application of the information contained in this book. Individual results may vary, and the information is not intended to diagnose, treat, cure, or prevent any medical condition.

SCAN THE QR CODE AND IMMEDIATELY ACCESS YOUR 3 SPECIAL BONUSES IN DIGITAL FORMAT!

TABLE OF CONTENTS

INTRODUCTION

Starting the journey to manage your diabetes is more than just altering your diet; it's a full lifestyle change that can significantly enhance your well-being, especially after 60. This book is created to be your guide, filled with over 2,000 days of simple, quick, low-carb, and low-sugar recipes designed to help you master pre-diabetes and Type 2 diabetes.

In addition to recipes, you'll find essential advice on how to shop smartly, dine out without stress, and make lasting changes to your daily habits. This guide is not only about helping you manage your blood sugar levels but also about improving your overall quality of life.

Whether you're recently diagnosed or have been managing diabetes for some time, this book provides the tools and insights needed to take control of your health. It equips you with the information to make wise decisions by outlining the rationale behind each dietary guideline.

Keep in mind that each step you take in this book will bring you closer to living a life that is healthier and more alive. Let's begin this new chapter together, starting right now.

Understanding Diabetes After 60

As you age, your body undergoes various changes that can affect how it processes sugar, making diabetes management particularly crucial after . It's common for muscle mass to decrease and for fat to increase, which affects how your body uses insulin. This period of life may also bring about reductions in physical activity and metabolic rate. When combined, these variables may raise the chance of getting Type 2 diabetes or make pre-existing problems worse.

The first step to take charge is realizing the special difficulties associated with treating diabetes after the age of fifty. Diabetes isn't just about high blood sugar; it impacts various aspects of your health, including heart, kidney, and nerve functions. The good news is that with the right dietary choices and lifestyle changes, you can significantly influence how your body manages this condition.

This section of the book dives deep into what happens to your body as it ages and how these changes impact your diabetes. It explores strategies for adapting your management techniques to fit your current lifestyle and body's needs. You'll learn how important it is to monitor your blood glucose levels consistently and how diet and exercise play pivotal roles in stabilizing those levels.

With a clear understanding of the physiological changes and their implications, you'll be better equipped to tackle diabetes management head-on. With this information at hand, you'll discover that it's simpler to make wise choices that lead to a better existence.

The Importance of Diet in Managing Diabetes

Particularly after the age of 60, diet is crucial to the management of diabetes. Your insulin sensitivity, blood sugar levels, and general health are all directly impacted by what you consume. Maintaining blood sugar control and preventing the many negative effects of diabetes, such as kidney damage, nerve pain, and heart disease, require eating a diet low in sugar and carbohydrates.

A well-planned diabetic diet does more than limit harmful elements; it also ensures you receive the nutrients necessary for sustaining energy, repairing tissues, and maintaining immune function. It focuses on balancing macronutrients—carbohydrates, proteins, and fats—to optimize blood sugar control and promote a healthy weight. This balance is crucial, as it affects how quickly glucose is released into your bloodstream and how your body manages insulin production.

Consuming a variety of high-fiber meals, such as veggies, whole grains, and legumes, can also help to keep blood sugar levels more consistent throughout the day by slowing down the absorption of sugar. Similarly, choosing healthy fats and lean proteins can aid in satiety and overall cardiovascular health.

This section of the book will delve into how specific dietary choices can create a robust framework for managing diabetes effectively. You'll learn how to construct meals that support your health goals, minimize your risk of diabetes-related complications, and still enjoy the pleasures of eating. By understanding the crucial link between diet and diabetes control, you'll be empowered to make choices that foster long-term health and stability.

PART I

GETTING STARTED

This part of the book is designed to set the stage for your new dietary approach, offering you the basic knowledge and tools needed to understand and implement a diabetic-friendly diet. Here, we'll cover the essentials of what constitutes a balanced diabetic diet, how to manage your macronutrients, and the importance of choosing the right foods for optimal blood sugar control.

Although the first steps may seem overwhelming, this section will walk you through each one in an easy-to-understand manner. We aim to equip you with the confidence and know-how to make informed decisions about your diet from the very first day. Let's begin this journey with a clear path forward, ensuring you have a strong foundation on which to build lasting health improvements.

The Basics of a Diabetic Diet

Understanding the basics of a diabetic diet is crucial for anyone looking to manage their diabetes effectively, especially as they age. This diet is not just about restricting certain foods but about creating a balanced, nutritious eating plan that supports blood sugar control and overall health.

A cornerstone of a diabetic diet is the balanced intake of macronutrients—carbohydrates, proteins, and fats. Carbs have the biggest influence on blood sugar levels. It's important to choose high-quality, complex carbohydrates that provide energy and fiber. These include whole grains like oats and quinoa, legumes, and non-starchy vegetables. These foods' fiber helps reduce blood glucose increases by slowing down the absorption of sugar.

Since our muscle mass continues to decline with age, protein becomes even more crucial for maintaining and growing new muscle. An appropriate amount of protein should be included in each meal in order to maintain muscle mass and control blood sugar levels. Fish, poultry, eggs, and plant-based meals like lentils and chickpeas are good sources of protein.

Good fats are essential for both heart health and for making it easier for vitamins to be absorbed. Good sources of healthful fats are olive oil, avocados, nuts, and seeds. These fats do not directly impact blood sugar levels and can help to satiate hunger, which assists in weight management.

Understanding the glycemic index (GI) and glycemic load (GL) of foods can also aid in managing diabetes. The GI gauges how rapidly a food item raises blood sugar levels, whereas the GL takes the food's carbohydrate content into account. Foods with a low GI and GL are preferable as they cause a slower and smaller rise in blood sugar levels. Examples include most non-starchy vegetables, some fruits like berries and apples, and whole grains.

Portion control is another vital aspect of a diabetic diet. Overindulging in food, even nutritious ones, can result in increased blood sugar and weight gain. Using measuring cups, a food scale, or even just smaller plates can help you control portions effectively.

Blood sugar levels can be greatly impacted by the time and frequency of meals. Eating at regular intervals helps to avoid significant fluctuations in blood sugar. Most dietitians recommend three meals a day with healthy snacks in between to keep metabolism consistent and prevent the intense hunger that can lead to overeating.

A diverse diet is not only more enjoyable but also ensures a range of nutrients to support overall health. Each food group offers unique benefits, so including a variety of foods is crucial. This promotes a healthier, livelier lifestyle in addition to helping to control blood sugar levels. By following these fundamental guidelines, people can better control their diabetes and make educated dietary decisions.

Carbs, Proteins, and Fats: Balancing for Blood Sugar Control

Efficient management of diabetes requires a diet that strikes a balance between carbohydrates, proteins, and fats—especially if you're over 60. Both general health and stable blood sugar levels depend on this equilibrium.

Carbohydrates are often seen as the enemy of those with diabetes, but it's more about the type and quantity of carbs consumed. Choose complex carbs with lots of fiber; they digest more slowly and don't cause blood sugar spikes. Foods like whole grains, legumes, vegetables, and some fruits fall into this category. It's also helpful to space out your carbohydrate intake throughout the day and watch portion sizes in order to keep your blood sugar levels steady.

In example, as you age and your muscle mass naturally decreases, proteins play a critical role in both maintaining and repairing your body. Because they don't directly affect blood sugar levels, proteins are a reliable source of energy. Every meal should include a source of lean protein, such as beans, fish, chicken, or tofu, to help you feel full and content without sharply raising your blood sugar levels.

A diabetic diet should contain fats, but it's important to choose the proper kinds of fats. Diabetes raises the risk of heart disease, thus it's critical to control blood cholesterol and maintain cardiac function. Good sources of unsaturated fats include avocados, almonds, seeds, and olive oil. However, fats are calorie-dense, so moderating intake is necessary to maintain a healthy weight.

The way that carbohydrates, proteins, and fats interact with one another affects how well your body stores energy and regulates blood sugar. For example, consuming carbs along with protein and fats can help reduce blood sugar spikes and provide more consistent energy. This is because they slow down the absorption of sugar into the bloodstream.

Moreover, understanding how each of these macronutrients affects your body can help you make informed choices about what to eat and when. For example, you know you'll be more active on a particular day. In that case, you should increase your intake of carbohydrates to provide enough energy, balancing it with proteins and fats to ensure that your blood sugar remains steady.

This well-rounded strategy not only supports blood sugar regulation but also a general healthier way of living. You may better control your diabetes and lower your risk of complications by paying attention to the quality of the macronutrients and their ratio in your meals. This will set the stage for an older you that is healthier.

The Low-Carb, Low-Sugar Approach

Adopting a low-carb, low-sugar approach is a fundamental strategy for managing diabetes, particularly after the age of 60, when metabolic changes can make blood sugar control more challenging. This dietary strategy focuses on reducing the intake of carbohydrates, particularly those that impact blood sugar levels quickly and significantly, such as sugars and refined starches.

Why Low-Carb and Low-Sugar?

Carbohydrates are the primary macronutrients that raise blood glucose levels. By limiting these, especially the simpler forms like sugars, you can help keep your blood glucose levels more stable. This is crucial in diabetes management, where the primary goal is to prevent the peaks and troughs that can lead to long-term complications.

A low-carb diet doesn't mean eliminating carbohydrates entirely but rather choosing them wisely. The idea is to eat carbohydrates that release glucose into the bloodstream gradually through slow digestion. These include fibrous vegetables, whole grains, and some fruits. The reduction in sugar and refined carbohydrates, like white bread, pasta, and pastries, helps avoid sudden spikes in blood sugar.

Benefits Beyond Blood Sugar Control

The benefits of a low-carb, low-sugar diet extend beyond just managing blood sugar levels. Additionally, it helps support weight loss efforts and good weight maintenance. People who are overweight are considerably more likely to acquire type 2 diabetes, and losing weight will increase your body's sensitivity to insulin, which will help you better control your blood sugar levels.

This strategy also frequently results in improvements to other health indices, such as blood pressure, HDL (good) cholesterol, and triglyceride levels.

Practical Implementation

Implementing a low-carb, low-sugar diet can start with simple swaps and mindful eating practices:

- Nuts or yogurt are better snack alternatives to sugary ones.
- Select items made from whole grains rather than refined grains.
- Incorporate more non-starchy vegetables into meals.
- To find out if processed foods have any hidden sugars, carefully examine food labels.

It's also important to consider the overall balance of your meals. To further slow down the release of glucose into the blood and maintain a sensation of fullness and satisfaction, it can be beneficial to pair your meals with a source of protein and healthy fat.

Considerations for the Long Term

While the benefits are clear, this dietary approach requires consideration of your overall nutritional needs and personal preferences to make it sustainable in the long term. It's not just about reducing carb intake but about making thoughtful food choices that support your health goals.

You can get individualized advice to make sure you are getting all the nutrients you need while on a low-carb, low-sugar diet by speaking with a healthcare professional or dietitian. This customized advice is crucial because each individual's health status, lifestyle, and dietary preferences are unique.

Adopting this approach involves more than just dietary changes; it's about embracing a lifestyle that enhances your health and overall quality of life. You can effectively control your diabetes and live a healthy, active life well into the age of 60 with careful preparation and consideration.

Shopping Smart

When managing diabetes, especially after 60, shopping smart becomes crucial for maintaining a healthy diet. Learning how to shop at the grocery store and make the best decisions will greatly enhance your ability to regulate your blood sugar and overall health. Here's how to make the most out of your shopping trips:

Start with a plan before you even step into the grocery store. Making a list based on your weekly meals and snacks can help you avoid impulse buys that might be less healthy. This list should focus on fresh produce, lean proteins, whole grains, and healthy fats—key components of a diabetic-friendly diet.

Reading labels is an essential skill in smart shopping. Pay close attention to not only the nutritional facts but also the ingredient list. Foods with a short, recognizable list of ingredients are typically less processed. Look for items with low added sugars and low sodium levels, as both can adversely affect your diabetes management. The nutritional labels will also help you understand the portion sizes and carbohydrate content, which are critical for managing your meal planning.

As much as possible, choose whole foods over processed ones. Lean meats, whole grains, and fresh produce are healthier options than prepackaged meals and snacks, which frequently have high concentrations of bad fats and hidden sugars. If fresh produce isn't available, frozen vegetables and fruits are a good alternative as they are usually packed at peak freshness and contain no added sugars or salts.

Shopping the store's perimeter first is another piece of advice. This is where the freshest foods like fruits, vegetables, dairy products, and meats are typically located. Processed foods are usually found in the central aisles of the store, so if you fill your cart from the perimeter first, you'll make better choices and have less room for less healthy options.

Think about the products' origins and quality. Organic and locally sourced foods can sometimes offer higher nutritional quality, though they might be more expensive. Balancing your budget with the quality of food can be part of your strategy for long-term health management.

Finally, don't shop when you're hungry. When you shop when you're hungry, your cravings may influence your decisions more than your true nutritional requirements. A small, healthy snack before heading to the grocery store can prevent this.

By adopting these smart shopping habits, you can ensure that you're bringing home the best foods to help manage your diabetes. This proactive approach to grocery shopping not only supports your dietary needs but also enhances your overall approach to health as you age.

How to Read Labels

Learning how to read labels effectively is a vital skill for managing diabetes, particularly as nutritional information can often seem complex and overwhelming. Understanding what to look for on these labels can help you make informed decisions about the foods you consume, ensuring they align with your dietary needs for managing blood sugar levels.

Examine the portion size specified on the label first. This is crucial because all the nutritional information provided relates to this specific amount of food. Comparing this to the amount you actually consume can help you accurately calculate your intake of calories, carbohydrates, and other nutrients.

Next, focus on the carbohydrates section of the label. This part includes total carbohydrates, dietary fiber, sugars, and added sugars. Pay close attention to the overall amount of carbohydrates and fiber for the control of diabetes. Fiber helps to regulate blood sugar rises because it slows down the digestion of carbs. By subtracting the grams of fiber from the total grams of carbohydrates, you may determine your "net carbs," which is a more precise estimate of the quantity of carbohydrates that will impact your blood sugar levels.

Added sugars are also critical to watch. These are sugars that are added to foods during processing and can quickly raise blood sugar levels. The lower the amount of added sugars, the better the food is for blood sugar control. Choosing foods with minimal or no added sugars can significantly benefit your diabetes management.

Also, assess the fats on the label, particularly trans fats and saturated fats. While these do not directly impact blood sugar levels, they can influence heart health, which is a major concern for those with diabetes. Opt for foods low in these fats to help maintain a healthy heart.

Protein content is another important factor. Protein can aid in satiety and the maintenance of muscle growth, and unlike carbohydrates, it does not increase blood sugar levels. Checking the protein content can help you balance your meals effectively.

Lastly, think about the concentration of salt. heavy blood pressure is another risk factor for cardiovascular disease, and a diet heavy in sodium exacerbates this condition. Thus, controlling your sodium consumption is also essential for general health, especially when you have diabetes.

You may choose foods that will support your overall health goals and assist maintain stable blood sugar levels by learning how to read nutrition labels. This skill enhances your ability to control your diet actively and make choices that contribute positively to your diabetes management.

Diabetic Food Shopping List

Creating a diabetic food shopping list is a strategic way to ensure you stock up on nutritious, beneficial foods that help manage blood sugar levels and overall health. This list can guide your grocery shopping, making it quicker, easier, and more effective in maintaining a diabetic-friendly diet. Here's a comprehensive list of foods to consider:

Vegetables: Focus on non-starchy vegetables as they are low in carbohydrates and high in fiber, vitamins, and minerals. Incorporate a range of hues and styles, including:

- Spinach and other leafy greens
- Broccoli
- Cauliflower
- Bell peppers
- Carrots
- Zucchini
- Cucumbers

Fruits: Choose fruits that are lower in sugar and high in fiber. While all fruits can fit into a diabetic diet, some options are particularly good:

- Berries (strawberries, blueberries, raspberries)
- Apples
- Pears
- Oranges
- Peaches
- Plums

Proteins: Choose lean protein sources instead of carbs, as they don't immediately raise blood sugar levels and are essential for preserving muscle mass:

- Chicken breast
- Turkey

Fish, especially fatty types like salmon and mackerel which are high in omega-3 fatty acids

- Eggs
- Tofu and other soy products
- Lentils and beans

Whole Grains: Whole grains provide essential nutrients and fiber, which helps control blood sugar levels:

- Brown rice
- Quinoa
- Whole oats
- Barley
- Whole grain bread and pasta

Dairy and Dairy Alternatives: Look for low-fat and low-sugar options to add calcium and protein to your diet without excessive sugar or fat:

- Low-fat milk or unsweetened almond, soy, or oat milk
- Low-fat yogurt, especially Greek yogurt, is higher in protein
- Cheese, particularly low-fat varieties

Healthy Fats: These are vital for heart health and can help to satiate hunger, making it easier to manage your diet:

Avocados

Nuts and seeds, including chia seeds, flaxseeds, walnuts, and almonds

- Olive oil and other vegetable oils

Herbs and Spices: These add flavor without contributing sugar or significant calories:

- Garlic
- Turmeric
- Cinnamon
- Ginger
- Fresh herbs like basil, cilantro, and parsley

Condiments and Sweeteners: Choose options that add flavor without added sugars or unhealthy fats:

- Mustard
- Vinegar (apple cider, balsamic)
- Low-sodium soy sauce
- Use erythritol or stevia as sweeteners rather than sugar.

This shopping list covers the basics for a well-rounded, nutritious diet that can help manage diabetes effectively. By sticking to this list, you can make meal planning easier and ensure that you're eating foods that support your health goals.

PART II

BEYOND THE PLATE

P art II of this guide, "Beyond the Plate," takes your journey with diabetes management a step further. While diet is foundational in controlling blood sugar levels, there are other crucial aspects to consider that can significantly enhance your ability to manage diabetes effectively. This section explores how lifestyle choices, particularly dining out, using supplements, and understanding their role in your diet, extend the principles of healthy eating into every part of your life. Here, we delve into practical strategies for maintaining your dietary goals even in challenging situations, ensuring that your efforts in managing diabetes are comprehensive and fit seamlessly into your broader lifestyle.

Dining Out with Diabetes

Dining out with diabetes doesn't have to be a daunting experience. With a bit of planning and knowledge about what to look for, you can enjoy meals at restaurants without compromising your blood sugar control. Here are strategies to help you maintain your dietary management while enjoying dining out.

Before you head out, it's wise to do some research. Many restaurants offer their menus online, allowing you to decide beforehand what's suitable for your dietary needs. Look for meals that are balanced, featuring good sources of proteins, vegetables, and whole grains, while being mindful of high-carb and high-sugar options.

Understanding menu terms can go a long way in helping you make healthy choices. Dishes labeled as steamed, broiled, grilled, baked, or roasted are typically less likely to be high in unhealthy fats and calories. On the other hand, terms like fried, breaded, smothered, creamy, or crispy are indicators that the food may be higher in carbohydrates, fats, and calories.

Don't be shy about asking for dishes to be modified according to your dietary needs. Most restaurants are willing to accommodate requests such as dressing on the side, no added salt, or substituting a side of fries for a salad or extra vegetables. This can significantly reduce the amount of carbs, fat, and overall calories in your meal.

Restaurant portions are often much larger than what you might serve at home. Consider asking for a half portion or sharing a dish with someone else. Another strategy is to ask for a to-go box right away and place half of your meal in the box to avoid overeating.

Beverages can add a significant amount of sugar and calories to your meal. Opt for water, unsweetened tea, or a diet soda instead of sugary drinks. If you drink alcohol, choose options with fewer carbs like light beer or a glass of wine, and always keep moderation in mind as alcohol can affect blood sugar levels.

If you're on insulin or other medications that can cause hypoglycemia (low blood sugar), it's wise to check your blood sugar before and after eating out to see how different foods affect your glucose levels. This can help you better understand your body's response and plan for future dining experiences.

If you wish to have dessert, look for fruit-based options or share a dessert with the table. Some restaurants might offer smaller dessert portions or items specifically made with less sugar.

If dining out is a frequent part of your lifestyle, it becomes even more crucial to find a way to enjoy this part of your social life without letting it derail your health goals. Consistency in how you choose your meals and managing portions is key to integrating dining out into a diabetic-friendly lifestyle.

By employing these strategies, you can enjoy the social aspects of eating out while still keeping your diabetes management on track.

How to Choose a Restaurant

Choosing the right restaurant is a critical part of managing diabetes effectively when dining out. The choice of venue can greatly influence the types of food available and how accommodating the establishment may be to dietary restrictions. It's important to select places that offer a variety of healthy options and are known for their flexibility in customizing orders.

When selecting a restaurant, start by looking for places that emphasize fresh, whole foods. Restaurants that offer a variety of salads, grilled proteins, and abundant vegetable sides are often a good choice. These types of eateries are more likely to use fresh ingredients and simple, healthy cooking methods that don't add unnecessary fats and sugars to your meals. Ethnic restaurants, such as Mediterranean or Japanese, often offer a wide range of dishes that naturally align with a diabetic-friendly diet, such as dishes rich in vegetables, lean proteins, and whole grains.

Another tip is to seek out restaurants that are open about their cooking methods and ingredients. Many places now provide nutritional information on their menus, either online or on request in the restaurant. This transparency allows you to make informed decisions about what to order based on carbohydrate content, calorie count, and the presence of other nutrients. Some restaurants also highlight low-carb, low-fat, or low-sugar options, making it easier to adhere to your dietary needs.

Before deciding on a restaurant, it's also beneficial to read reviews from other diners, especially those who mention dietary restrictions. Reviews can provide insights into how accommodating a restaurant is when it comes to modifying dishes and if the staff is knowledgeable about the content of their menus. Additionally, calling the restaurant in advance to discuss your dietary needs can also be a proactive step. This not only helps you feel more comfortable about your options but also signals to the restaurant staff that you have specific dietary requirements, allowing them to prepare and provide suggestions that meet your needs.

Lastly, consider the overall dining environment and service quality, as a relaxed dining experience can also affect meal choices and enjoyment. Restaurants that are known for attentive service are more likely to take your dietary needs seriously and ensure that your dining experience is pleasant and aligned with your health goals. By carefully selecting a restaurant that supports your dietary needs, you can enjoy dining out without undue stress over managing your diabetes.

What to Order in Any Cuisine

Navigating restaurant menus to find diabetes-friendly options can be challenging, but knowing what to look for in any cuisine can make dining out a much easier and more enjoyable experience. Here's how you can make smart choices across various types of cuisines:

In Italian restaurants, the key is to avoid heavy pasta dishes and instead opt for protein-based meals. Look for grilled fish or chicken dishes, and consider substituting any pasta sides with a salad or extra vegetables. Italian cuisine often features a variety of seafood dishes which are excellent for a balanced meal. Also, don't hesitate to ask for tomato-based sauces rather than cream-based ones, as these are usually lower in fat and calories.

When dining at Mexican restaurants, the focus should be on avoiding fried items like tortilla chips and dishes heavy in cheese and sour cream. Instead, choose grilled options such as fajitas, which offer a mix of protein and vegetables. Opt for corn tortillas rather than flour tortillas since they are typically lower in carbs and calories, and request additional vegetables or a side salad to replace higher-carb items like rice and beans.

Chinese cuisine can be tricky due to the prevalence of sugar and high-sodium sauces. When possible, choose steamed dishes like steamed chicken or shrimp with vegetables and ask for the sauce on the side so you can control the amount you consume. Dishes such as moo goo gai pan and other steamed vegetable and lean protein dishes are usually safe bets. Avoid fried options like egg rolls and sweet sauces like those found in orange chicken or General Tso's chicken.

For Indian dining, it's beneficial to steer clear of creamy curries and dishes that contain hidden sugars. Opt for tandoori-cooked dishes, which are marinated and cooked in a clay oven without additional fat or sugars. Accompany these with a side of vegetables instead of higher-carb rice or naan. Dal dishes (lentil-based) are also a good option as lentils provide a healthy dose of fiber

In Japanese restaurants, sushi can be a good option, but it's best to avoid rolls that contain fried ingredients or creamy sauces. Sashimi (slices of raw fish without rice) or nigiri (fish with a small ball of rice) can be good choices. Also, edamame and miso soup are great starters that are low in carbohydrates.

American cuisine often includes a wide variety of options, making it easier to find something suitable. Look for grilled or baked meats and seafood. Salads are a staple in many American restaurants but be cautious with dressings, which can be high in sugar and calories. Ask for the dressing on the side and use sparingly.

By applying these general guidelines, you can enjoy a meal out in almost any type of restaurant without worrying about disrupting your blood sugar control. Making informed choices and asking for slight modifications where necessary will allow you to manage your diabetes effectively while still enjoying a diverse range of flavors and dishes.

Tips for Eating Out

Eating out when managing diabetes requires a thoughtful approach to ensure your meals align with your health goals. Here are some practical tips to help you maintain control over your blood sugar while enjoying dining out.

Firstly, it's beneficial to familiarize yourself with the menu ahead of time. Many restaurants offer their menus online, allowing you to plan your meal before you even arrive. This preparation prevents the pressure of making a quick decision at the table and helps you avoid choices that might not be conducive to your dietary needs.

When ordering, don't hesitate to communicate clearly with your server about your dietary preferences. Most restaurants are willing to accommodate modifications to dishes, such as dressing on the side, no added salt, or substituting starchy sides like fries or mashed potatoes with extra vegetables or a salad. This not only ensures the meal fits within your dietary requirements but also often leads to a fresher, healthier dish.

Portion control is crucial, as restaurant portions can be significantly larger than what you might serve at home. Consider ordering a starter as your main course or sharing a main dish with a dining companion. Alternatively, you can ask for half of your meal to be boxed up before it's brought to the table, which helps avoid the temptation to overeat.

Be mindful of hidden sugars and fats, particularly in sauces and dressings. Opting for meals that are grilled, baked, or steamed rather than fried can drastically reduce unwanted calories and fats. Additionally, asking for sauces and dressings on the side allows you to control the amount you consume.

It's also important to think about how the timing of your meal fits with your overall daily food intake and medication schedule. If you take insulin or other medications that can cause hypoglycemia, planning your restaurant meals around your medication times can help keep your blood sugar levels stable.

Finally, stay hydrated by drinking water throughout your meal, which can help you avoid mistaking thirst for hunger and overeating. Water is also a much better choice than sugary drinks, which can cause a rapid increase in blood sugar levels. If you enjoy alcoholic beverages, opt for a light beer, a glass of wine, or a spirit with a sugar-free mixer, and always drink in moderation as alcohol can affect blood sugar levels.

By keeping these tips in mind, you can enjoy dining out without compromising your health, ensuring that each meal out is both enjoyable and in line with your dietary management of diabetes.

Supplements and Your Diet

When managing diabetes, incorporating supplements into your diet can sometimes offer additional benefits, but it's important to approach this area with caution and informed understanding. Supplements should never replace prescribed medication or the nutritional benefits of a well-rounded diet, but in certain cases, they can help fill nutritional gaps or address specific dietary deficiencies.

It's essential to first discuss any supplement plans with a healthcare provider, particularly if you're managing diabetes. Some supplements can interact with diabetic medications and affect blood sugar levels, either lowering them too much or interfering with the medication's effectiveness.

Among the supplements commonly considered by those with diabetes, omega-3 fatty acids are often recommended. These are beneficial for heart health, which is particularly important because diabetes increases the risk of heart disease. Omega-3 supplements, such as fish oil, can help reduce triglycerides and promote overall cardiovascular health.

Another beneficial supplement is magnesium, which many people with diabetes are deficient in. Magnesium plays a vital role in glucose control and insulin sensitivity, and supplementing with it can help manage these factors more effectively if you are not getting enough from your diet.

Chromium is also frequently discussed in relation to diabetes. It's believed to enhance the action of insulin and has been studied for its potential to improve blood sugar control, although results are mixed, and more research is needed to confirm these benefits.

Vitamin D levels are another consideration, as they are often low in people with diabetes. Vitamin D is crucial for bone health and has been linked to improved insulin sensitivity. Ensuring adequate vitamin D, either through diet, sunlight, or supplements, can support diabetes management.

It's also worth considering the role of herbal supplements like cinnamon, which has been touted for its potential to lower blood sugar levels. However, the evidence is varied, and cinnamon should not be used as a substitute for diabetes medication.

When considering supplements, always look for products that have been independently tested by reputable sources for purity and potency. This ensures that the supplements are free from contaminants and actually contain the ingredients listed on the label.

Maintaining open communication with your healthcare provider about all supplements you consider is vital. This ensures your entire healthcare team is informed and can provide the best advice based on your overall health needs and specific diabetic condition.

When Diet Isn't Enough: What Supplements Can Help

When managing diabetes through diet alone isn't sufficient, supplements can sometimes play a supportive role in enhancing your overall health and blood sugar control. However, it's crucial to approach supplementation under the guidance of healthcare professionals to ensure safe and effective use, particularly as some supplements can interact with diabetes medications.

One common supplement considered by many with diabetes is alpha-lipoic acid, known for its antioxidant properties. Alpha-lipoic acid has been studied for its ability to help improve insulin sensitivity and reduce symptoms of diabetic neuropathy, such as pain, tingling, and numbness in the limbs.

Another supportive supplement is berberine, a compound found in several plants. Research suggests that berberine can help lower blood sugar levels to a similar extent as some diabetes drugs. It works by improving insulin sensitivity and increasing glycolysis, helping to break down sugars inside cells.

Biotin, often taken in combination with chromium, has been studied for its potential to enhance glucose management. Biotin by itself can influence blood sugar levels by facilitating the activity of insulin and supporting various metabolic functions involving glucose.

Coenzyme Q10, or CoQ10, is another supplement that may be beneficial for individuals with diabetes. CoQ10 levels are often lower in people with diabetes. This nutrient helps cells produce energy and may be beneficial in counteracting the side effects of statin medications, commonly prescribed for heart health, which can sometimes increase a person's risk of developing diabetes.

Vitamin B12 supplementation might also be necessary, especially for those on metformin, a common diabetes medication that can reduce the absorption of B12, potentially leading to deficiency over time. A B12 supplement can prevent deficiency symptoms, which include fatigue, memory impairment, and neuropathy.

It is important to note that while these supplements can aid in managing diabetes, they are not a cure and should not replace conventional treatments prescribed by a doctor. Moreover, supplements can vary widely in quality, so choosing products certified by a reputable third-party organization is crucial to ensure safety and efficacy.

Ultimately, supplements may serve as a valuable tool in your diabetes management strategy, but they should be used as part of a comprehensive approach that includes dietary adjustments, physical activity, regular monitoring of blood sugar levels, and medications as prescribed by your healthcare provider. Always consult with your healthcare team before starting any new supplement to ensure it is appropriate for your specific health needs and conditions.

The Do's and Don'ts of Supplements

Navigating the world of supplements, especially when managing diabetes, requires careful consideration to ensure safety and effectiveness. Here's a comprehensive overview of the do's and don'ts when it comes to incorporating supplements into your diabetes care routine.

Do's:

Do consult with your healthcare provider before starting any new supplement. This is essential because some supplements can interact with diabetes medications or affect blood sugar levels in unpredictable ways. Your healthcare provider can help you understand which supplements might benefit you based on your specific health needs and conditions.

Do choose high-quality supplements from reputable manufacturers. Look for products that have been verified by third-party organizations such as USP (United States Pharmacopeia), NSF International, or ConsumerLab. These groups test supplements to ensure that they contain the ingredients listed on the label and do not contain harmful levels of contaminants.

Do educate yourself about each supplement you consider taking. Understand what the supplement is supposed to do, the evidence supporting its use, and the recommended dosages. Knowing these can help you make informed decisions and discuss them knowledgeably with your healthcare provider.

Do monitor your blood sugar levels closely if you start taking a new supplement that is known to affect glucose metabolism. Supplements like cinnamon, alpha-lipoic acid, and berberine may require adjustments to your diabetes medication or insulin therapy, so careful monitoring is essential.

Do'store supplements properly to maintain their efficacy. Most supplements should be kept in a cool, dry place to prevent degradation of their active ingredients.

Don'ts:

Don't assume more is better. Follow dosage recommendations strictly. Taking more than the advised amount of a supplement can lead to unwanted side effects and potentially serious health risks.

Don't use supplements to replace prescribed diabetes medication. Supplements should not be considered substitutes for the medications prescribed by your healthcare provider. They should only be used to complement your existing treatment plan.

Don't fall for "miracle cures" or overhyped cure-alls advertised on the internet or social media. If something sounds too good to be true, it likely is. Reliable health improvements require realistic, scientifically backed methods, not quick fixes.

Don't mix multiple supplements without approval from a healthcare professional, as some combinations can lead to harmful interactions or counteract each other's effects.

Don't neglect to tell all your healthcare providers about all supplements you are taking, so they can manage your overall care safely and effectively. This includes doctors, pharmacists, and dietitians.

By following these do's and don'ts, you can safely incorporate supplements into your diabetes management plan, potentially enhancing your overall health outcomes while avoiding common pitfalls associated with supplement use.

PART III

THE RECIPES

Part III of this guide, "The Recipes," is designed to bring the principles of a diabetic-friendly diet to life through delicious, nutritious meals that fit seamlessly into your daily routine. Whether you're looking for a quick breakfast, a satisfying lunch, or a hearty dinner, this section provides a variety of recipes that cater to your dietary needs while keeping your blood sugar levels in check. Each recipe has been carefully crafted to ensure it is not only healthy but also flavorful and easy to prepare. From comforting classics to innovative dishes, these recipes will help you enjoy a diverse and enjoyable diet that supports your diabetes management goals.

CHAPTER 1

BREAKFASTS TO KICKSTART YOUR DAY

Chapter 1, "Breakfasts to Kickstart Your Day," is all about beginning your mornings with meals that energize and stabilize your blood sugar. We recognize that a hearty, nutritious breakfast sets the tone for the day, especially for managing diabetes. This chapter offers a variety of recipes ranging from quick, on-the-go options to leisurely, comforting meals, ensuring that no matter how much time you have in the morning, you can start your day right. Each recipe is designed to provide a balanced mix of carbohydrates, proteins, and fats to keep your energy levels steady and your cravings at bay until your next meal.

Avocado Toast with Poached Eggs

Ingredients:

- 2 slices of whole grain bread
- 1 ripe avocado
- 2 eggs
- Salt and pepper to taste
- Optional toppings: cherry tomatoes, arugula, red pepper flakes

37

Directions:

1. Begin by poaching the eggs. Bring a pot of water to a gentle simmer, add a small splash of vinegar, and create a gentle whirlpool. Crack each egg into a small bowl and gently tip them into the simmering water. Cook for about 3-4 minutes for soft poached eggs or longer for firmer yolks. Remove with a slotted spoon and set aside on a warm plate.
2. While the eggs are poaching, toast the bread slices to your desired crispness.
3. Halve the avocado and remove the pit. Scoop the avocado flesh into a bowl, mash it with a fork, and season with salt and pepper.
4. Spread the mashed avocado evenly on each slice of toasted bread.
5. Carefully place a poached egg on top of each avocado-covered toast.
6. Add optional toppings like sliced cherry tomatoes, arugula, or a sprinkle of red pepper flakes for extra flavor.
7. Serve immediately.

Nutritional Values (per serving):

- Calories: 290
- Fat: 20g
- Carbohydrates: 22g
- Protein: 12g

Greek Yogurt Parfait with Berries and Nuts

Ingredients:

- 1 cup Greek yogurt (plain, unsweetened)
- 1/2 cup mixed berries (blueberries, strawberries, raspberries)
- 1/4 cup mixed nuts (almonds, walnuts, pecans), roughly chopped
- Optional: 1 tablespoon honey or a sprinkle of cinnamon for added flavor

Directions:

1. If using honey or cinnamon, mix it into the Greek yogurt until well combined. You can adjust the amount based on your taste preferences and dietary needs.
2. In a serving glass or bowl, start by layering half of the Greek yogurt at the bottom.
3. Add a layer of mixed berries over the yogurt.
4. Sprinkle half of the chopped nuts over the berries.
5. Repeat the layering with the remaining yogurt, berries, and nuts to create a visually appealing parfait.
6. Serve immediately or chill in the refrigerator for up to an hour before serving if you prefer a colder parfait.

Nutritional Values (per serving):

- Calories: 345
- Fat: 18g
- Carbohydrates: 25g
- Protein: 20g

Spinach and Feta Omelet

Ingredients:

- 2 large eggs
- 1 cup fresh spinach, chopped
- 1/4 cup feta cheese, crumbled
- 1 tablespoon olive oil
- Salt and pepper to taste
- Optional: diced tomatoes or onions for added flavor

Directions:

1. In a mixing bowl, whisk the eggs with salt and pepper until well combined.
2. Heat the olive oil in a non-stick skillet over medium heat.
3. Add the optional diced tomatoes or onions to the skillet and sauté for about 2 minutes until soft.
4. Add the chopped spinach to the skillet and cook until just wilted, about 1-2 minutes.
5. Pour the whisked eggs over the spinach in the skillet, allowing the eggs to spread evenly.
6. Sprinkle the crumbled feta cheese evenly over the top of the eggs.
7. Cover the skillet with a lid and let the omelet cook for 3-4 minutes, or until the eggs are set and the feta is slightly melted.
8. Carefully fold the omelet in half with a spatula and slide onto a plate.
9. Serve immediately.

Nutritional Values (per serving):

- Calories: 290
- Fat: 23g
- Carbohydrates: 3g
- Protein: 17g

Cinnamon Almond Flour Pancakes

Ingredients:

- 1 cup almond flour
- 2 large eggs
- 1/4 cup water or unsweetened almond milk
- 1 teaspoon cinnamon
- 1 tablespoon stevia or sweetener of choice
- 1 teaspoon vanilla extract
- 1/2 teaspoon baking powder
- Pinch of salt
- Olive oil or coconut oil for cooking

Directions:

1. In a large bowl, combine the almond flour, cinnamon, stevia (or another sweetener), baking powder, and a pinch of salt.
2. In another bowl, whisk together the eggs, water (or almond milk), and vanilla extract until well blended.
3. Pour the wet ingredients into the dry ingredients and stir until just combined. The batter should be thick but pourable; adjust the consistency with a little more water or almond milk if needed.
4. Heat a non-stick skillet over medium heat and brush with a small amount of oil.
5. Pour 1/4 cup of batter for each pancake onto the hot skillet. Cook for 2-3 minutes until the edges start to look set and bubbles form on the surface, then flip carefully and cook for another 2-3 minutes on the other side until golden and cooked through.
6. Repeat with the remaining batter, adding more oil to the skillet as needed.
7. Serve the pancakes hot with your choice of toppings, such as fresh berries, a dollop of Greek yogurt, or a drizzle of sugar-free syrup.

Nutritional Values (per serving, based on four pancakes):

- Calories: 315
- Fat: 25g
- Carbohydrates: 10g (Net carbs: 6g)
- Protein: 14g

Chia Seed Pudding with Coconut Milk

Ingredients:

- 1/4 cup chia seeds
- 1 cup coconut milk (unsweetened)
- 1 tablespoon honey or a sweetener of choice (adjust to taste)
- 1/2 teaspoon vanilla extract
- Optional toppings: fresh berries, sliced almonds, or shredded coconut

Directions:

1. In a mixing bowl, combine the chia seeds, coconut milk, honey (or another sweetener), and vanilla extract. Stir thoroughly to mix all the ingredients.
2. Cover the bowl with a lid or plastic wrap and refrigerate for at least 2 hours, preferably overnight. This allows the chia seeds to absorb the liquid and swell up, creating a pudding-like consistency.
3. Once the pudding has set, stir it well. If the pudding is too thick, you can add a little more coconut milk to reach your desired consistency.
4. Serve the chia seed pudding in individual bowls or glasses. Add your choice of toppings like fresh berries, sliced almonds, or shredded coconut right before serving for added texture and flavor.

Nutritional Values (per serving):

- Calories: 265
- Fat: 19g
- Carbohydrates: 21g
- Fiber: 10g
- Protein: 5g

Low-Carb Blueberry Muffins

Ingredients:

- 1 and 1/2 cups almond flour
- 1/4 cup coconut flour
- 1/2 teaspoon baking powder
- 1/4 teaspoon salt
- 1/3 cup granulated sweetener of choice (e.g., erythritol or monk fruit sweetener)
- 3 large eggs
- 1/3 cup unsweetened almond milk
- 1/4 cup coconut oil, melted
- 1 teaspoon vanilla extract
- 1/2 cup fresh or frozen blueberries

Directions:

1. Preheat your oven to 350°F (175°C) and line a muffin tin with paper liners or grease with cooking spray.
2. In a large mixing bowl, combine almond flour, coconut flour, baking powder, salt, and sweetener.
3. In another bowl, whisk together eggs, almond milk, melted coconut oil, and vanilla extract until well combined.
4. Pour the wet ingredients into the dry ingredients and mix until just combined, being careful not to overmix.
5. Gently fold in the blueberries.
6. Distribute the batter evenly among the prepared muffin cups, filling each about three-quarters full.
7. Bake in the preheated oven for 20-25 minutes, or until a toothpick inserted into the center of a muffin comes out clean or with just a few moist crumbs.
8. Remove from the oven and let the muffins cool in the pan for 5 minutes, then transfer them to a wire rack to cool completely.

Nutritional Values (per muffin):

- Calories: 160
- Fat: 14g
- Carbohydrates: 8g
- Fiber: 3g
- Net Carbs: 5g
- Protein: 5g

Smoked Salmon and Cream Cheese Bagel (Low-Carb Bagel)

Ingredients:

- 2 low-carb bagels (store-bought or homemade)
- 4 ounces smoked salmon
- 2 tablespoons cream cheese, softened
- 1 tablespoon capers
- 1/4 red onion, thinly sliced
- Fresh dill for garnish
- Black pepper to taste

Directions:

1. Slice the low-carb bagels in half and toast them to your preference.
2. Spread each half generously with cream cheese.
3. Layer the smoked salmon slices evenly over the cream cheese on each bagel half.
4. Sprinkle capers and red onion slices over the smoked salmon.
5. Garnish with fresh dill and a sprinkle of black pepper according to your taste.
6. Serve immediately, enjoying the blend of flavors and textures.

Nutritional Values (per serving, 1 bagel with toppings):

- Calories: 290
- Fat: 18g

- Carbohydrates: 13g (Net carbs may vary based on the type of low-carb bagel used)
- Protein: 24g

Vegetable Hash with Eggs

Ingredients:

- 2 tablespoons olive oil
- 1 medium sweet potato, peeled and diced
- 1 red bell pepper, diced
- 1 small zucchini, diced
- 1/2 red onion, diced
- 2 cloves garlic, minced
- 1 teaspoon smoked paprika
- Salt and pepper to taste
- 4 large eggs
- Optional garnish: chopped fresh parsley or chives

Directions:

1. Heat olive oil in a large skillet over medium heat. Add the diced sweet potato and cook for about 5 minutes, stirring occasionally, until they begin to soften.
2. Add the red bell pepper, zucchini, and red onion to the skillet. Continue cooking for another 5-7 minutes, or until all vegetables are tender and starting to brown.
3. Stir in the minced garlic, smoked paprika, salt, and pepper, cooking for an additional minute until fragrant.
4. Make four wells in the vegetable hash and crack an egg into each well. Cover the skillet with a lid and let the eggs cook for 5-8 minutes, or until the egg whites are set but the yolks are still runny (cook longer if you prefer firmer yolks).

5. Remove from heat, garnish with chopped parsley or chives if using, and serve immediately.

Nutritional Values (per serving):

- Calories: 250
- Fat: 15g
- Carbohydrates: 18g
- Fiber: 3g
- Protein: 12g

Keto Breakfast Sandwich

Ingredients:

- 2 large eggs
- 1 tablespoon heavy cream
- Salt and pepper to taste
- 2 tablespoons unsalted butter
- 2 slices of cheddar cheese
- 4 slices of cooked bacon
- 2 large portobello mushroom caps, stems removed and cleaned

Directions:

1. In a small bowl, whisk together the eggs, heavy cream, salt, and pepper until well combined.
2. Heat a non-stick skillet over medium heat and melt one tablespoon of butter. Pour in the egg mixture, allowing it to spread out into a thin omelet. Cook for about 2-3 minutes on one side, then flip and cook for another 1-2 minutes. Place the slices of cheddar cheese on top of the omelet during the last minute of cooking to let it melt. Once cooked, fold the omelet into a size that will fit the mushrooms, and set aside.
3. In the same skillet, add the remaining tablespoon of butter. Place the portobello mushroom caps gill-side down and cook for about 3-4 minutes on each side, or until they are fully cooked and have released most of their moisture.
4. Assemble the sandwich by placing half of the cooked bacon on one of the mushroom caps, top with the folded egg and cheese omelet, add the remaining bacon, and cap it with the other mushroom. Press gently to secure the layers.
5. Serve immediately while warm.

Nutritional Values (per sandwich):

- Calories: 590
- Fat: 48g
- Carbohydrates: 8g
- Fiber: 2g
- Net Carbs: 6g
- Protein: 34g

Protein-Packed Smoothie Bowl

Ingredients:

- 1 scoop of your favorite protein powder (vanilla or unflavored works best)
- 1/2 cup Greek yogurt (unsweetened)
- 1/2 banana, sliced
- 1/2 cup mixed berries (such as strawberries, blueberries, and raspberries)
- 1/4 cup almond milk (unsweetened)
- 1 tablespoon chia seeds
- Optional toppings: sliced almonds, coconut flakes, additional berries, a spoonful of nut butter

Directions:

1. In a blender, combine the protein powder, Greek yogurt, banana, mixed

berries, and almond milk. Blend on high until smooth and creamy.

2. Pour the smoothie mixture into a bowl. The consistency should be thick enough to hold toppings.

3. Sprinkle the chia seeds evenly over the top of the smoothie.

4. Add your choice of optional toppings such as sliced almonds, coconut flakes, additional berries, or a dollop of nut butter for extra flavor and texture.

5. Serve immediately and enjoy this nourishing and filling protein-packed smoothie bowl as a revitalizing breakfast or a refreshing post-workout meal.

Nutritional Values (per serving):

- Calories: 350
- Fat: 10g
- Carbohydrates: 30g
- Fiber: 8g
- Protein: 30g

Almond Butter and Banana Shake

Ingredients:

- 1 large ripe banana
- 2 tablespoons almond butter
- 1 cup almond milk (unsweetened)
- 1/2 teaspoon vanilla extract
- 1 scoop of vanilla protein powder (optional for extra protein)
- Ice cubes (optional, for a thicker shake)

Directions:

1. Peel the banana and place it in a blender.
2. Add the almond butter, almond milk, vanilla extract, and protein powder if using.

3. If you prefer a colder, thicker shake, add a handful of ice cubes to the blender.

4. Blend all the ingredients on high speed until smooth and creamy.

5. Pour the shake into a glass and serve immediately.

Nutritional Values (per serving):

- Calories: 380
- Fat: 18g
- Carbohydrates: 35g
- Fiber: 6g
- Protein: 20g (varies if you add protein powder)

Cottage Cheese with Pineapple

Ingredients:

- 1 cup low-fat cottage cheese
- 1/2 cup chopped fresh pineapple (or canned pineapple chunks in juice, drained)
- Optional: a sprinkle of cinnamon or honey for added flavor

Directions:

1. Place the cottage cheese in a serving bowl.

2. Top the cottage cheese with the chopped pineapple, evenly distributing it across the surface.

3. If desired, add a sprinkle of cinnamon or a drizzle of honey over the top for extra flavor.

4. Serve immediately, enjoying the creamy texture of the cottage cheese with the sweet, tangy burst of pineapple.

Nutritional Values (per serving):

- Calories: 220
- Fat: 2g
- Carbohydrates: 20g
- Fiber: 1g
- Protein: 26g

Baked Avocado Eggs

Ingredients:

- 2 ripe avocados
- 4 small eggs
- Salt and pepper to taste
- Optional garnishes: chopped chives, parsley, or a sprinkle of paprika

Directions:

1. Preheat your oven to 425°F (220°C).
2. Slice the avocados in half and remove the pits. Scoop out a little more avocado flesh to make room for the eggs, being careful not to break through the bottom.
3. Place the avocado halves on a baking tray, and stabilize them with a small piece of foil if they wobble.
4. Crack an egg into each avocado half. It's easiest to do this by cracking each egg into a small cup first, then gently pouring it into the avocado to prevent the yolk from breaking.
5. Season with salt and pepper, and add any additional spices or herbs if desired.
6. Carefully place the baking tray in the oven and bake for 15-20 minutes, or until the eggs are cooked to your liking.
7. Remove from the oven and garnish with chopped chives, parsley, or a sprinkle of paprika before serving.

Nutritional Values (per serving, 1/2 an avocado with egg):

- Calories: 230
- Fat: 19g
- Carbohydrates: 8g
- Fiber: 6g
- Protein: 9g

Zucchini Bread (Sugar-Free)

Ingredients:

- 1 1/2 cups almond flour
- 1/2 cup coconut flour
- 1 teaspoon baking soda
- 1/2 teaspoon baking powder
- 1/2 teaspoon salt
- 1 teaspoon ground cinnamon
- 1/2 teaspoon ground nutmeg
- 3 large eggs
- 1/4 cup melted coconut oil
- 1/4 cup unsweetened applesauce
- 1 teaspoon vanilla extract
- 1 1/2 cups grated zucchini (squeezed to remove excess moisture)
- 1/4 cup chopped walnuts or pecans (optional)

Directions:

1. Preheat your oven to 350°F (175°C) and grease a 9x5-inch loaf pan or line it with parchment paper.
2. In a large mixing bowl, combine the almond flour, coconut flour, baking soda, baking powder, salt, cinnamon, and nutmeg. Mix well.
3. In another bowl, whisk together the eggs, melted coconut oil, unsweetened applesauce, and vanilla extract until well combined.

4. Add the wet ingredients to the dry ingredients and stir until just combined.
5. Fold in the grated zucchini and chopped nuts (if using) until evenly distributed.
6. Pour the batter into the prepared loaf pan and smooth the top with a spatula.
7. Bake in the preheated oven for 45-50 minutes, or until a toothpick inserted into the center comes out clean.
8. Allow the zucchini bread to cool in the pan for about 10 minutes, then transfer it to a wire rack to cool completely before slicing.

Nutritional Values (per slice, based on 12 slices):

- Calories: 180
- Fat: 14g
- Carbohydrates: 9g
- Fiber: 4g
- Protein: 5g

Turkey Sausage Breakfast Burrito (Low-Carb Wrap)

Ingredients:

- 4 low-carb tortillas or wraps
- 1/2 pound ground turkey sausage
- 4 large eggs
- 1/4 cup unsweetened almond milk
- 1/2 cup shredded cheddar cheese
- 1 small bell pepper, diced
- 1 small onion, diced
- 1 tablespoon olive oil
- Salt and pepper to taste
- Optional toppings: salsa, avocado slices, chopped cilantro

Directions:

1. In a large skillet, heat the olive oil over medium heat. Add the diced onion and bell pepper, sautéing until they are softened, about 5 minutes.
2. Add the ground turkey sausage to the skillet, breaking it up with a spoon. Cook until browned and fully cooked through, about 7-10 minutes. Season with salt and pepper to taste. Remove the sausage and vegetable mixture from the skillet and set aside.
3. In a mixing bowl, whisk together the eggs and almond milk until well combined.
4. In the same skillet, over medium heat, pour the egg mixture in and cook, stirring frequently, until the eggs are scrambled and just set.
5. Return the sausage and vegetable mixture to the skillet with the eggs, stirring to combine. Remove from heat.
6. Warm the low-carb tortillas according to package instructions.
7. To assemble the burritos, lay each tortilla flat and spoon an equal portion of the egg and sausage mixture onto the center of each.
8. Sprinkle shredded cheddar cheese over the top of the egg mixture.
9. Roll the tortillas tightly, folding in the sides as you go to form a burrito.
10. If desired, lightly toast the burritos in a skillet for 1-2 minutes on each side to crisp the tortilla and melt the cheese further.
11. Serve immediately, with optional toppings like salsa, avocado slices, or chopped cilantro for added flavor.

Nutritional Values (per burrito):

- Calories: 350
- Fat: 22g
- Carbohydrates: 10g (Net carbs may vary based on the type of low-carb wrap used)
- Protein: 25g

Steel-Cut Oats with Apples

Ingredients:

- 1 cup steel-cut oats
- 4 cups water or unsweetened almond milk
- 1 medium apple, peeled, cored, and diced
- 1 teaspoon ground cinnamon
- 1/2 teaspoon vanilla extract
- 1 tablespoon chia seeds
- Optional toppings: chopped nuts, raisins, or a drizzle of honey

Directions:

1. In a medium saucepan, bring the water or unsweetened almond milk to a boil.
2. Add the steel-cut oats, reduce the heat to low, and let them simmer. Cook for about 20-30 minutes, stirring occasionally, until the oats reach your desired consistency.
3. While the oats are cooking, in a small skillet over medium heat, add the diced apple and ground cinnamon. Cook for about 5 minutes, stirring frequently, until the apples are tender.
4. Once the oats are cooked, stir in the vanilla extract and chia seeds.
5. Add the cooked apples to the oats and mix well.
6. Serve the oatmeal in bowls and add your favorite optional toppings, such as chopped nuts, raisins, or a drizzle of honey for extra sweetness and texture.

Nutritional Values (per serving):

- Calories: 220
- Fat: 5g
- Carbohydrates: 38g
- Fiber: 8g
- Protein: 6g

Spinach and Mushroom Breakfast Casserole

Ingredients:

- 1 tablespoon olive oil
- 1 medium onion, diced
- 2 cups fresh mushrooms, sliced
- 4 cups fresh spinach leaves
- 8 large eggs
- 1/2 cup milk (unsweetened almond milk or regular milk)
- 1 cup shredded mozzarella cheese
- Salt and pepper to taste
- 1/2 teaspoon garlic powder
- 1/4 teaspoon nutmeg
- Optional: chopped fresh herbs like parsley or chives for garnish

Directions:

1. Preheat your oven to 350°F (175°C). Grease a 9x13-inch baking dish with a bit of olive oil or cooking spray.
2. In a large skillet, heat the olive oil over medium heat. Add the diced onion and cook until softened, about 5 minutes.
3. Add the sliced mushrooms to the skillet and cook for another 5 minutes, or until the mushrooms are tender and have released their moisture.

4. Add the fresh spinach to the skillet and cook until wilted, about 2-3 minutes. Remove from heat and set aside.
5. In a large mixing bowl, whisk together the eggs, milk, salt, pepper, garlic powder, and nutmeg until well combined.
6. Stir in the shredded mozzarella cheese and the sautéed vegetables, mixing thoroughly.
7. Pour the mixture into the prepared baking dish, spreading it out evenly.
8. Bake in the preheated oven for 30-35 minutes, or until the casserole is set and lightly golden on top.
9. Remove from the oven and let it cool for a few minutes before slicing.
10. Garnish with chopped fresh herbs if desired, and serve warm.

Nutritional Values (per serving, based on 8 servings):

- Calories: 190
- Fat: 12g
- Carbohydrates: 5g
- Fiber: 1g
- Protein: 14g

Flaxseed and Walnut Porridge

Ingredients:

- 1/4 cup ground flaxseed
- 1/4 cup chopped walnuts
- 1 cup unsweetened almond milk (or your preferred milk)
- 1 tablespoon chia seeds
- 1 teaspoon ground cinnamon
- 1 teaspoon vanilla extract
- Optional toppings: fresh berries, sliced banana, a drizzle of honey or maple syrup

Directions:

1. In a small saucepan, combine the ground flaxseed, chopped walnuts, chia seeds, and ground cinnamon.
2. Pour in the unsweetened almond milk and stir well to combine.
3. Place the saucepan over medium heat and cook, stirring frequently, until the mixture thickens to a porridge-like consistency, about 5-7 minutes.
4. Remove the saucepan from heat and stir in the vanilla extract.
5. Let the porridge sit for a minute to allow the flavors to meld and the chia seeds to fully absorb the liquid.
6. Serve the porridge in bowls, adding your favorite optional toppings like fresh berries, sliced banana, or a drizzle of honey or maple syrup for extra flavor and sweetness.

Nutritional Values (per serving):

- Calories: 320
- Fat: 25g
- Carbohydrates: 12g
- Fiber: 10g
- Protein: 9g

Tomato and Basil Frittata

Ingredients:

- 8 large eggs
- 1/4 cup milk (unsweetened almond milk or regular milk)
- Salt and pepper to taste

- 1 tablespoon olive oil
- 1 cup cherry tomatoes, halved
- 1/4 cup fresh basil leaves, chopped
- 1/2 cup shredded mozzarella cheese
- 1/4 cup grated Parmesan cheese
- Optional: additional fresh basil leaves for garnish

Directions:

1. Preheat your oven to 375°F (190°C).
2. In a large bowl, whisk together the eggs, milk, salt, and pepper until well combined.
3. Heat the olive oil in an ovenproof skillet over medium heat. Add the cherry tomatoes and cook for about 3-4 minutes until they start to soften.
4. Stir in the chopped basil and cook for another minute.
5. Pour the egg mixture over the tomatoes and basil in the skillet, tilting the pan to ensure the eggs are evenly distributed.
6. Sprinkle the shredded mozzarella and grated Parmesan cheese evenly over the top.
7. Cook on the stovetop for about 2-3 minutes, just until the edges start to set.
8. Transfer the skillet to the preheated oven and bake for 15-20 minutes, or until the frittata is fully set and slightly golden on top.
9. Remove the frittata from the oven and let it cool for a few minutes before slicing.
10. Garnish with additional fresh basil leaves if desired, and serve warm.

Nutritional Values (per serving, based on 6 servings):

- Calories: 210
- Fat: 15g
- Carbohydrates: 3g
- Fiber: 1g
- Protein: 15g

Raspberry Almond Muffins

Ingredients:

- 1 1/2 cups almond flour
- 1/2 cup coconut flour
- 1 teaspoon baking powder
- 1/2 teaspoon baking soda
- 1/4 teaspoon salt
- 3 large eggs
- 1/3 cup honey or a sugar substitute
- 1/3 cup unsweetened almond milk
- 1/4 cup melted coconut oil
- 1 teaspoon vanilla extract
- 1 cup fresh raspberries
- 1/4 cup sliced almonds

Directions:

1. Preheat your oven to 350°F (175°C) and line a muffin tin with paper liners or grease with cooking spray.
2. In a large mixing bowl, combine the almond flour, coconut flour, baking powder, baking soda, and salt. Mix well to ensure there are no lumps.
3. In another bowl, whisk together the eggs, honey (or sugar substitute), almond milk, melted coconut oil, and vanilla extract until well combined.
4. Pour the wet ingredients into the dry ingredients and stir until just combined. Be careful not to overmix.
5. Gently fold in the fresh raspberries, taking care not to crush them.
6. Divide the batter evenly among the prepared muffin cups, filling each about three-quarters full.

7. Sprinkle the sliced almonds on top of each muffin.

8. Bake in the preheated oven for 20-25 minutes, or until a toothpick inserted into the center of a muffin comes out clean.

9. Remove the muffins from the oven and let them cool in the pan for about 5 minutes, then transfer them to a wire rack to cool completely.

Nutritional Values (per muffin, based on 12 muffins):

- Calories: 170
- Fat: 13g
- Carbohydrates: 10g
- Fiber: 4g
- Protein: 6g

Coconut Yogurt and Mixed Berries

Ingredients:

- 1 cup coconut yogurt (unsweetened)
- 1/2 cup mixed berries (such as strawberries, blueberries, raspberries, and blackberries)
- 1 tablespoon chia seeds
- 1 tablespoon unsweetened shredded coconut
- 1 teaspoon honey or a sugar substitute (optional, for added sweetness)
- Optional toppings: sliced almonds, granola, or fresh mint leaves

Directions:

1. In a serving bowl, place the coconut yogurt as the base.
2. Top the yogurt with the mixed berries, distributing them evenly.
3. Sprinkle the chia seeds and shredded coconut over the berries.

4. If desired, drizzle with honey or a sugar substitute for added sweetness.

5. Add any optional toppings such as sliced almonds, granola, or fresh mint leaves for extra texture and flavor.

6. Serve immediately and enjoy this refreshing and nutritious breakfast or snack.

Nutritional Values (per serving):

- Calories: 220
- Fat: 12g
- Carbohydrates: 18g
- Fiber: 6g
- Protein: 5g

Low-Carb Granola

Ingredients:

- 1 cup almonds, roughly chopped
- 1 cup walnuts, roughly chopped
- 1 cup pecans, roughly chopped
- 1/2 cup unsweetened shredded coconut
- 1/4 cup chia seeds
- 1/4 cup flaxseed meal
- 1/4 cup sunflower seeds
- 1/4 cup pumpkin seeds
- 2 tablespoons coconut oil, melted
- 2 tablespoons sugar-free maple syrup or a sweetener of choice
- 1 teaspoon vanilla extract
- 1 teaspoon ground cinnamon
- 1/2 teaspoon salt

Directions:

1. Preheat your oven to 300°F (150°C) and line a baking sheet with parchment paper.

2. In a large mixing bowl, combine the chopped almonds, walnuts, pecans, shredded coconut, chia seeds, flaxseed meal, sunflower seeds, and pumpkin seeds.

3. In a small bowl, whisk together the melted coconut oil, sugar-free maple syrup (or sweetener of choice), vanilla extract, ground cinnamon, and salt.

4. Pour the wet mixture over the nut and seed mixture, stirring well to ensure everything is evenly coated.

5. Spread the granola mixture in an even layer on the prepared baking sheet.

6. Bake in the preheated oven for 20-25 minutes, stirring halfway through to ensure even baking, until the granola is golden brown and fragrant.

7. Remove from the oven and let the granola cool completely on the baking sheet. It will become crispier as it cools.

8. Once cooled, transfer the granola to an airtight container for storage.

Nutritional Values (per serving, based on 12 servings):

- Calories: 200
- Fat: 18g
- Carbohydrates: 6g
- Fiber: 4g
- Protein: 5g

Pepper and Egg White Scramble

Ingredients:

- 6 large egg whites
- 1 red bell pepper, diced
- 1 green bell pepper, diced
- 1 small onion, diced
- 1 tablespoon olive oil
- Salt and pepper to taste
- Optional: chopped fresh parsley or chives for garnish

Directions:

1. In a large bowl, whisk the egg whites until they are slightly frothy.

2. Heat the olive oil in a non-stick skillet over medium heat.

3. Add the diced onion to the skillet and cook for about 3-4 minutes, or until it begins to soften.

4. Add the diced red and green bell peppers to the skillet. Continue cooking for another 5-7 minutes, or until the vegetables are tender.

5. Pour the egg whites into the skillet, stirring gently to combine with the vegetables.

6. Cook the egg whites, stirring frequently, until they are fully cooked and no longer runny, about 3-4 minutes.

7. Season with salt and pepper to taste.

8. Remove from heat and garnish with chopped fresh parsley or chives if desired.

9. Serve immediately, enjoying this light and nutritious scramble for breakfast or brunch.

Nutritional Values (per serving, based on 2 servings):

- Calories: 120
- Fat: 5g
- Carbohydrates: 6g
- Fiber: 2g
- Protein: 12g

Protein Pancakes

Ingredients:

- 1/2 cup rolled oats
- 1/2 cup cottage cheese
- 2 large eggs
- 1 scoop vanilla protein powder
- 1 teaspoon vanilla extract
- 1/2 teaspoon baking powder
- 1/4 teaspoon cinnamon
- Optional toppings: fresh berries, sugar-free syrup, almond butter

Directions:

1. In a blender, combine the rolled oats, cottage cheese, eggs, protein powder, vanilla extract, baking powder, and cinnamon. Blend until the mixture is smooth and well combined.
2. Heat a non-stick skillet or griddle over medium heat and lightly grease with cooking spray or a small amount of oil.
3. Pour about 1/4 cup of the batter onto the skillet for each pancake. Cook for 2-3 minutes, or until bubbles form on the surface and the edges begin to set.
4. Flip the pancakes and cook for an additional 2-3 minutes, or until golden brown and cooked through.
5. Repeat with the remaining batter, greasing the skillet as needed.
6. Serve the pancakes warm with your choice of optional toppings like fresh berries, sugar-free syrup, or almond butter.

Nutritional Values (per serving, based on 2 servings):

- Calories: 290
- Fat: 8g
- Carbohydrates: 20g
- Fiber: 3g
- Protein: 30g

Turkey Bacon and Avocado Wrap

Ingredients:

- 4 slices of turkey bacon
- 1 ripe avocado
- 1 tablespoon lemon juice
- Salt and pepper to taste
- 2 low-carb tortillas or wraps
- 1/2 cup shredded lettuce
- 1 small tomato, diced
- Optional: a few slices of red onion or a sprinkle of hot sauce

Directions:

1. Cook the turkey bacon in a skillet over medium heat until crispy. Remove from the skillet and place on a paper towel to drain excess grease.
2. In a small bowl, mash the avocado with the lemon juice, and season with salt and pepper to taste.
3. Lay out the low-carb tortillas on a flat surface. Spread half of the mashed avocado mixture evenly over each tortilla.
4. Layer the shredded lettuce, diced tomato, and cooked turkey bacon slices on top of the avocado spread.
5. Add any optional ingredients such as red onion slices or a sprinkle of hot sauce for extra flavor.
6. Roll up the tortillas tightly to form wraps, folding in the sides as you go to secure the fillings.
7. Slice each wrap in half and serve immediately.

Nutritional Values (per wrap):

- Calories: 280
- Fat: 18g

- Carbohydrates: 16g (Net carbs may vary based on the type of low-carb wrap used)
- Fiber: 10g

- Protein: 16g

CHAPTER 2
SATISFYING LUNCHES

Whether you're at home, at work, or on the go, these recipes are crafted to be both convenient and delicious, ensuring that your midday meal is both enjoyable and supportive of your dietary goals. From hearty salads to flavorful wraps and warm, comforting soups, each dish is packed with nutrients and balanced to help you maintain stable blood sugar levels throughout the afternoon. Dive into these creative lunch ideas and discover how easy it can be to enjoy healthy, fulfilling meals every day.

Grilled Chicken Caesar Salad

Ingredients:

- 2 boneless, skinless chicken breasts
- 1 tablespoon olive oil
- Salt and pepper to taste
- 6 cups romaine lettuce, chopped
- 1/4 cup grated Parmesan cheese
- 1/2 cup cherry tomatoes, halved
- 1/4 cup Caesar dressing (store-bought or homemade)
- Optional: croutons or sliced avocado for extra texture and flavor

Directions:

1. Preheat your grill to medium-high heat. Brush the chicken breasts with olive oil and season with salt and pepper.
2. Grill the chicken for 6-7 minutes on each side, or until fully cooked and the internal temperature reaches 165°F (74°C). Remove from the grill and let the chicken rest for a few minutes before slicing.
3. In a large salad bowl, combine the chopped romaine lettuce, grated Parmesan cheese, and cherry tomatoes.
4. Slice the grilled chicken breasts into thin strips and add them to the salad.
5. Drizzle the Caesar dressing over the salad and toss to coat all the ingredients evenly.
6. Serve immediately, garnished with croutons or sliced avocado if desired.

Nutritional Values (per serving, based on 2 servings):

- Calories: 350
- Fat: 22g
- Carbohydrates: 10g
- Fiber: 4g
- Protein: 30g

Turkey and Avocado Roll-Ups

Ingredients:

- 8 slices of deli turkey breast
- 1 ripe avocado
- 1 tablespoon lemon juice
- Salt and pepper to taste
- 1/2 cup shredded lettuce
- 1 small tomato, thinly sliced
- Optional: a few slices of red onion or a sprinkle of hot sauce

Directions:

1. In a small bowl, mash the avocado with the lemon juice, and season with salt and pepper to taste.
2. Lay the turkey slices flat on a clean surface. Spread a thin layer of the mashed avocado mixture evenly over each slice of turkey.
3. Place a small amount of shredded lettuce and a slice of tomato on one end of each turkey slice.
4. Add any optional ingredients like red onion slices or a sprinkle of hot sauce for extra flavor.
5. Starting from the end with the lettuce and tomato, roll up each turkey slice tightly to form a roll-up.
6. Secure each roll-up with a toothpick if necessary, and serve immediately.

Nutritional Values (per roll-up, based on 4 servings):

- Calories: 150
- Fat: 10g
- Carbohydrates: 5g
- Fiber: 3g
- Protein: 12g

Quinoa and Black Bean Salad

Ingredients:

- 1 cup quinoa, rinsed
- 2 cups water
- 1 can (15 oz) black beans, drained and rinsed
- 1 cup cherry tomatoes, halved
- 1 red bell pepper, diced
- 1 small red onion, finely chopped
- 1/2 cup fresh cilantro, chopped
- 1/4 cup olive oil
- 2 tablespoons lime juice
- 1 teaspoon ground cumin
- Salt and pepper to taste
- Optional: diced avocado, corn kernels, or crumbled feta cheese for extra flavor

Directions:

1. In a medium saucepan, bring the quinoa and water to a boil. Reduce the heat to low, cover, and simmer for about 15 minutes, or until the quinoa is tender and the water is absorbed. Remove from heat and let it cool slightly.
2. In a large bowl, combine the cooked quinoa, black beans, cherry tomatoes, red bell pepper, red onion, and fresh cilantro.
3. In a small bowl, whisk together the olive oil, lime juice, ground cumin, salt, and pepper until well combined.
4. Pour the dressing over the quinoa and vegetable mixture, and toss to coat all the ingredients evenly.
5. Add any optional ingredients like diced avocado, corn kernels, or crumbled feta cheese for added texture and flavor.
6. Serve immediately or refrigerate for up to an hour to allow the flavors to meld.

Nutritional Values (per serving, based on 4 servings):

- Calories: 320
- Fat: 14g
- Carbohydrates: 40g
- Fiber: 8g
- Protein: 8g

Mediterranean Veggie Wrap (Low-Carb Wrap)

Ingredients:

- 2 low-carb tortillas or wraps
- 1/2 cup hummus (store-bought or homemade)
- 1/2 cup cucumber, thinly sliced
- 1/2 cup cherry tomatoes, halved
- 1/4 cup red onion, thinly sliced
- 1/4 cup Kalamata olives, pitted and sliced
- 1/4 cup crumbled feta cheese
- 1/2 cup fresh spinach leaves
- 2 tablespoons fresh parsley, chopped
- 1 tablespoon olive oil
- 1 tablespoon lemon juice
- Salt and pepper to taste

Directions:

1. In a small bowl, whisk together the olive oil, lemon juice, salt, and pepper to make a simple dressing.
2. Lay out the low-carb tortillas on a flat surface. Spread an even layer of hummus over each tortilla, leaving a small border around the edges.
3. Arrange the cucumber slices, cherry tomatoes, red onion, Kalamata olives, crumbled feta cheese, and fresh spinach leaves evenly over the hummus on each tortilla.
4. Drizzle the olive oil and lemon juice dressing over the vegetables.
5. Sprinkle the chopped fresh parsley over the top.
6. Roll up each tortilla tightly, folding in the sides as you go to secure the fillings.
7. Slice each wrap in half, and serve immediately.

Nutritional Values (per wrap):

- Calories: 300
- Fat: 18g
- Carbohydrates: 22g (Net carbs may vary based on the type of low-carb wrap used)
- Fiber: 8g
- Protein: 10g

Broccoli and Cheddar Soup

Ingredients:

- 4 cups fresh broccoli florets
- 1 medium onion, chopped
- 2 cloves garlic, minced
- 4 cups low-sodium chicken or vegetable broth
- 1 cup heavy cream
- 2 cups shredded sharp cheddar cheese
- 2 tablespoons butter
- 2 tablespoons olive oil
- Salt and pepper to taste
- Optional: a pinch of nutmeg for added flavor

Directions:

1. In a large pot, heat the olive oil and butter over medium heat. Add the chopped onion and cook until softened, about 5 minutes.
2. Add the minced garlic and cook for another minute until fragrant.
3. Stir in the broccoli florets and cook for 3-4 minutes, until they begin to soften.
4. Pour in the low-sodium chicken or vegetable broth and bring to a boil. Reduce the heat and let it simmer for about 15 minutes, or until the broccoli is tender.

5. Using an immersion blender, blend the soup until smooth. If you prefer a chunkier texture, blend only part of the soup and leave some broccoli florets whole.
6. Stir in the heavy cream and shredded cheddar cheese, and continue to cook over low heat until the cheese is fully melted and the soup is heated through.
7. Season with salt and pepper to taste. Add a pinch of nutmeg if desired for extra flavor.
8. Serve hot, garnished with extra shredded cheddar cheese or a dollop of sour cream if desired.

Nutritional Values (per serving, based on 6 servings):

- Calories: 300
- Fat: 24g
- Carbohydrates: 10g
- Fiber: 3g
- Protein: 12g

Shrimp and Avocado Salad

Ingredients:

- 1 pound large shrimp, peeled and deveined
- 1 tablespoon olive oil
- 2 avocados, diced
- 1 cup cherry tomatoes, halved
- 1 small red onion, finely chopped
- 1/4 cup fresh cilantro, chopped
- 1 jalapeño, seeded and finely chopped (optional)
- 2 tablespoons lime juice
- Salt and pepper to taste
- Optional: mixed greens or lettuce for serving

Directions:

1. In a large skillet, heat the olive oil over medium-high heat. Add the shrimp and cook for 2-3 minutes on each side, or until the shrimp are pink and opaque. Remove from heat and let cool slightly.
2. In a large bowl, combine the diced avocados, cherry tomatoes, red onion, cilantro, and jalapeño (if using).
3. Add the cooked shrimp to the bowl and gently toss to combine.
4. Drizzle the lime juice over the salad and season with salt and pepper to taste.
5. Serve the shrimp and avocado salad on its own or over a bed of mixed greens or lettuce for added freshness and crunch.

Nutritional Values (per serving, based on 4 servings):

- Calories: 300
- Fat: 20g
- Carbohydrates: 12g
- Fiber: 7g
- Protein: 20g

Beef Lettuce Wraps

Ingredients:

- 1 pound ground beef (preferably lean)
- 1 tablespoon olive oil
- 1 small onion, finely chopped
- 2 cloves garlic, minced
- 1 tablespoon soy sauce (or tamari for gluten-free)
- 1 tablespoon hoisin sauce (optional, for added sweetness)
- 1 teaspoon fresh ginger, grated
- 1/2 teaspoon red pepper flakes (optional, for heat)

- 1/2 cup water chestnuts, chopped
- 1/4 cup green onions, chopped
- 1/4 cup fresh cilantro, chopped
- 1 head of lettuce (such as Bibb, butter, or iceberg), leaves separated
- Optional toppings: shredded carrots, chopped peanuts, or sesame seeds

Directions:

1. In a large skillet, heat the olive oil over medium-high heat. Add the finely chopped onion and cook until softened, about 5 minutes.
2. Add the minced garlic and grated ginger to the skillet, and cook for another minute until fragrant.
3. Add the ground beef to the skillet, breaking it up with a spoon. Cook until the beef is browned and cooked through, about 7-10 minutes.
4. Stir in the soy sauce, hoisin sauce (if using), and red pepper flakes. Cook for another 2-3 minutes, allowing the flavors to meld.
5. Add the chopped water chestnuts and cook for an additional minute.
6. Remove the skillet from heat and stir in the chopped green onions and cilantro.
7. To assemble the wraps, spoon a portion of the beef mixture onto the center of each lettuce leaf.
8. Add optional toppings like shredded carrots, chopped peanuts, or sesame seeds for extra texture and flavor.
9. Serve immediately, allowing everyone to wrap their lettuce leaves around the beef filling.

Nutritional Values (per serving, based on 4 servings):

- Calories: 310

- Fat: 20g
- Carbohydrates: 10g
- Fiber: 3g
- Protein: 25g

Spinach and Goat Cheese Stuffed Portobello Mushrooms

Ingredients:

- 4 large portobello mushrooms, stems removed and gills scraped out
- 2 tablespoons olive oil
- 1 small onion, finely chopped
- 2 cloves garlic, minced
- 4 cups fresh spinach, chopped
- 4 ounces goat cheese, crumbled
- 1/4 cup grated Parmesan cheese
- Salt and pepper to taste
- 1/4 teaspoon red pepper flakes (optional)
- Fresh parsley, chopped, for garnish

Directions:

1. Preheat your oven to 375°F (190°C). Line a baking sheet with parchment paper.
2. Brush the portobello mushrooms with 1 tablespoon of olive oil and place them on the prepared baking sheet, gill side up. Season with salt and pepper.
3. In a large skillet, heat the remaining 1 tablespoon of olive oil over medium heat. Add the finely chopped onion and cook until softened, about 5 minutes.
4. Add the minced garlic to the skillet and cook for another minute until fragrant.
5. Add the chopped spinach to the skillet and cook until wilted, about 2-3 minutes. Season with salt, pepper, and red pepper flakes if using.

6. Remove the skillet from heat and stir in the crumbled goat cheese until well combined.
7. Spoon the spinach and goat cheese mixture evenly into each portobello mushroom cap.
8. Sprinkle the grated Parmesan cheese over the top of each stuffed mushroom.
9. Bake in the preheated oven for 20-25 minutes, or until the mushrooms are tender and the cheese is golden and bubbly.
10. Remove from the oven and let cool for a few minutes. Garnish with chopped fresh parsley before serving.

Nutritional Values (per serving, based on 4 servings):

- Calories: 220
- Fat: 16g
- Carbohydrates: 10g
- Fiber: 3g
- Protein: 10g

Tuna Salad Stuffed Tomatoes

Ingredients:

- 4 large tomatoes
- 2 cans (5 oz each) tuna in water, drained
- 1/4 cup mayonnaise (or Greek yogurt for a lighter option)
- 1 tablespoon Dijon mustard
- 1 small celery stalk, finely chopped
- 1 small red onion, finely chopped
- 2 tablespoons fresh parsley, chopped
- 1 tablespoon capers (optional)
- 1 tablespoon lemon juice
- Salt and pepper to taste
- Optional garnish: fresh basil or dill

Directions:

1. Cut the tops off the tomatoes and carefully scoop out the insides using a spoon, creating a hollow cavity. Discard the seeds and pulp or save for another use.
2. In a medium bowl, combine the drained tuna, mayonnaise (or Greek yogurt), Dijon mustard, chopped celery, chopped red onion, chopped parsley, capers (if using), and lemon juice. Mix well until all ingredients are thoroughly combined.
3. Season the tuna salad with salt and pepper to taste.
4. Spoon the tuna salad mixture into each hollowed-out tomato, filling them generously.
5. Garnish with fresh basil or dill if desired.
6. Serve immediately, or chill in the refrigerator for up to an hour before serving for a cooler, refreshing dish.

Nutritional Values (per serving, based on 4 servings):

- Calories: 200
- Fat: 10g
- Carbohydrates: 10g
- Fiber: 3g
- Protein: 18g

Cauliflower Fried Rice

Ingredients:

- 1 medium head of cauliflower, riced (about 4 cups)
- 2 tablespoons olive oil
- 1 small onion, finely chopped
- 2 cloves garlic, minced
- 1 cup frozen peas and carrots, thawed
- 2 large eggs, lightly beaten

- 3 tablespoons soy sauce (or tamari for gluten-free)
- 1 tablespoon sesame oil
- 1/4 cup green onions, chopped
- Optional: 1/4 cup cooked chicken, shrimp, or tofu for added protein

Directions:

1. To rice the cauliflower, cut it into florets and pulse in a food processor until it resembles rice. Alternatively, you can grate the cauliflower using a box grater.
2. In a large skillet or wok, heat 1 tablespoon of olive oil over medium heat. Add the finely chopped onion and cook until softened, about 3-4 minutes.
3. Add the minced garlic to the skillet and cook for another minute until fragrant.
4. Increase the heat to medium-high and add the riced cauliflower to the skillet. Cook for about 5-7 minutes, stirring frequently, until the cauliflower is tender but not mushy.
5. Push the cauliflower mixture to one side of the skillet and add the remaining 1 tablespoon of olive oil to the other side. Pour the beaten eggs into the oil and scramble until fully cooked.
6. Stir the scrambled eggs into the cauliflower mixture, then add the thawed peas and carrots. Cook for an additional 2-3 minutes until the vegetables are heated through.
7. Pour the soy sauce and sesame oil over the cauliflower rice, stirring well to combine.
8. If using cooked chicken, shrimp, or tofu, add it to the skillet and cook until heated through.
9. Remove from heat and stir in the chopped green onions.
10. Serve immediately, garnished with additional green onions if desired.

Nutritional Values (per serving, based on 4 servings):

- Calories: 150
- Fat: 9g
- Carbohydrates: 10g
- Fiber: 4g
- Protein: 6g

Zucchini Noodle Pad Thai

Ingredients:

- 4 medium zucchini, spiralized into noodles
- 2 tablespoons olive oil
- 1 pound shrimp, peeled and deveined (or substitute with chicken or tofu)
- 2 cloves garlic, minced
- 1 small red bell pepper, thinly sliced
- 1 cup bean sprouts
- 2 large eggs, lightly beaten
- 1/4 cup green onions, chopped
- 1/4 cup fresh cilantro, chopped
- 1/4 cup chopped peanuts
- Lime wedges, for serving

Pad Thai Sauce:

- 3 tablespoons fish sauce
- 2 tablespoons soy sauce (or tamari for gluten-free)
- 2 tablespoons rice vinegar
- 2 tablespoons lime juice
- 1 tablespoon peanut butter
- 1 tablespoon erythritol or another sugar substitute

- 1 teaspoon chili garlic sauce (optional, for heat)

Directions:

1. In a small bowl, whisk together all the ingredients for the Pad Thai sauce until well combined. Set aside.
2. Heat 1 tablespoon of olive oil in a large skillet or wok over medium-high heat. Add the shrimp and cook until pink and opaque, about 2-3 minutes per side. Remove from the skillet and set aside.
3. In the same skillet, add the remaining 1 tablespoon of olive oil. Add the minced garlic and sliced red bell pepper, cooking for about 2-3 minutes until the pepper begins to soften.
4. Push the vegetables to one side of the skillet and pour the beaten eggs into the other side. Scramble the eggs until fully cooked, then stir them into the vegetables.
5. Add the spiralized zucchini noodles to the skillet and cook for about 2-3 minutes, tossing gently to combine with the vegetables and eggs. The zucchini noodles should be tender but not mushy.
6. Pour the Pad Thai sauce over the zucchini noodles and toss to coat evenly. Add the cooked shrimp and bean sprouts, stirring until everything is well mixed and heated through.
7. Remove from heat and stir in the chopped green onions and cilantro.
8. Serve immediately, garnished with chopped peanuts and lime wedges on the side.

Nutritional Values (per serving, based on 4 servings):

- Calories: 260
- Fat: 14g
- Carbohydrates: 12g
- Fiber: 4g
- Protein: 20g

Chicken and Vegetable Soup

Ingredients:

- 2 tablespoons olive oil
- 1 medium onion, chopped
- 2 cloves garlic, minced
- 3 carrots, peeled and sliced
- 3 celery stalks, sliced
- 1 zucchini, diced
- 1 yellow squash, diced
- 1 cup green beans, trimmed and cut into 1-inch pieces
- 1 pound boneless, skinless chicken breasts, diced
- 6 cups low-sodium chicken broth
- 1 teaspoon dried thyme
- 1 teaspoon dried basil
- 1/2 teaspoon dried oregano
- Salt and pepper to taste
- 2 cups fresh spinach leaves
- 1/4 cup fresh parsley, chopped

Directions:

1. In a large pot, heat the olive oil over medium heat. Add the chopped onion and cook until softened, about 5 minutes.
2. Add the minced garlic, carrots, and celery to the pot. Cook for an additional 5 minutes, stirring occasionally.
3. Stir in the diced zucchini, yellow squash, and green beans. Cook for another 3 minutes.
4. Add the diced chicken to the pot and cook until no longer pink, about 5-7 minutes.
5. Pour in the low-sodium chicken broth and bring the soup to a boil.

6. Reduce the heat to low and add the dried thyme, dried basil, dried oregano, salt, and pepper. Let the soup simmer for 20-25 minutes, or until the vegetables are tender and the chicken is fully cooked.
7. Stir in the fresh spinach leaves and cook for another 2-3 minutes until wilted.
8. Remove the pot from heat and stir in the chopped fresh parsley.
9. Serve the soup hot, garnished with additional parsley if desired.

Nutritional Values (per serving, based on 6 servings):

- Calories: 210
- Fat: 8g
- Carbohydrates: 14g
- Fiber: 4g
- Protein: 22g

Egg Salad on Rye Bread (Low-Carb Rye)

Ingredients:

- 6 large eggs
- 1/4 cup mayonnaise (or Greek yogurt for a lighter option)
- 1 tablespoon Dijon mustard
- 1 celery stalk, finely chopped
- 1 small red onion, finely chopped
- 1 tablespoon fresh dill, chopped
- 1 teaspoon lemon juice
- Salt and pepper to taste
- 4 slices of low-carb rye bread
- Optional: lettuce leaves or sliced tomato for serving

Directions:

1. Place the eggs in a medium saucepan and cover them with water. Bring the water to a boil over medium-high heat. Once boiling, cover the saucepan and remove it from the heat. Let the eggs sit for 10-12 minutes.
2. Drain the hot water and transfer the eggs to a bowl of ice water to cool. Once cooled, peel the eggs and chop them into small pieces.
3. In a large bowl, combine the chopped eggs, mayonnaise (or Greek yogurt), Dijon mustard, chopped celery, chopped red onion, fresh dill, and lemon juice. Mix until well combined.
4. Season the egg salad with salt and pepper to taste.
5. Toast the slices of low-carb rye bread to your desired level of crispness.
6. Spread the egg salad evenly over each slice of toasted rye bread.
7. Add optional toppings like lettuce leaves or sliced tomato for extra flavor and texture.
8. Serve immediately and enjoy.

Nutritional Values (per serving, based on 4 servings):

- Calories: 250
- Fat: 18g
- Carbohydrates: 12g (Net carbs may vary based on the type of low-carb rye bread used)
- Fiber: 4g
- Protein: 12g

Portobello Mushroom Pizza

Ingredients:

- 4 large portobello mushrooms, stems removed and gills scraped out
- 2 tablespoons olive oil

- 1/2 cup marinara sauce (sugar-free)
- 1 cup shredded mozzarella cheese
- 1/4 cup grated Parmesan cheese
- 1/2 cup cherry tomatoes, halved
- 1/4 cup sliced black olives
- 1/4 cup chopped fresh basil
- Salt and pepper to taste
- Optional: red pepper flakes, for a bit of heat

Directions:

1. Preheat your oven to 375°F (190°C). Line a baking sheet with parchment paper.
2. Brush the portobello mushrooms with olive oil on both sides and place them on the prepared baking sheet, gill side up. Season with a little salt and pepper.
3. Bake the mushrooms in the preheated oven for about 8-10 minutes to soften them slightly.
4. Remove the mushrooms from the oven and carefully drain any excess moisture that has collected in the caps.
5. Spread a couple of tablespoons of marinara sauce inside each mushroom cap.
6. Sprinkle the shredded mozzarella cheese and grated Parmesan cheese evenly over the sauce in each mushroom.
7. Top the mushrooms with cherry tomatoes and sliced black olives.
8. Return the mushrooms to the oven and bake for another 10-12 minutes, or until the cheese is melted and bubbly.
9. Remove the portobello mushroom pizzas from the oven and let them cool for a few minutes.
10. Garnish with chopped fresh basil and optional red pepper flakes before serving.

Nutritional Values (per serving, based on 4 servings):

- Calories: 220
- Fat: 15g
- Carbohydrates: 10g
- Fiber: 3g
- Protein: 12g

Balsamic Grilled Vegetables

Ingredients:

- 1 red bell pepper, cut into large chunks
- 1 yellow bell pepper, cut into large chunks
- 1 zucchini, sliced into thick rounds
- 1 yellow squash, sliced into thick rounds
- 1 red onion, cut into wedges
- 1 cup cherry tomatoes
- 2 tablespoons olive oil
- 3 tablespoons balsamic vinegar
- 2 cloves garlic, minced
- Salt and pepper to taste
- Fresh basil, chopped, for garnish

Directions:

1. Preheat your grill to medium-high heat.
2. In a large bowl, combine the olive oil, balsamic vinegar, minced garlic, salt, and pepper. Mix well.
3. Add the cut vegetables (bell peppers, zucchini, yellow squash, red onion, and cherry tomatoes) to the bowl and toss to coat them evenly with the balsamic mixture.
4. Place the vegetables on the preheated grill. Grill the vegetables for about 5-7 minutes on each side, or until they are tender and have nice grill marks.

5. Remove the vegetables from the grill and transfer them to a serving platter.
6. Garnish with chopped fresh basil before serving.

Nutritional Values (per serving, based on 4 servings):

- Calories: 120
- Fat: 7g
- Carbohydrates: 14g
- Fiber: 4g
- Protein: 2g

Chicken Taco Salad

Ingredients:

- 1 pound boneless, skinless chicken breasts
- 2 tablespoons olive oil
- 1 tablespoon taco seasoning
- 6 cups romaine lettuce, chopped
- 1 cup cherry tomatoes, halved
- 1/2 cup red onion, thinly sliced
- 1/2 cup black beans, drained and rinsed
- 1/2 cup corn kernels (fresh or frozen)
- 1 avocado, diced
- 1/4 cup shredded cheddar cheese
- 1/4 cup fresh cilantro, chopped
- Juice of 1 lime
- Salt and pepper to taste
- Optional toppings: sour cream, salsa, or crushed tortilla chips

Directions:

1. Preheat your grill or a skillet over medium-high heat.

2. Rub the chicken breasts with olive oil and sprinkle with taco seasoning, ensuring they are evenly coated.
3. Grill the chicken for about 6-7 minutes on each side, or until fully cooked and the internal temperature reaches 165°F (74°C). Remove from heat and let rest for a few minutes before slicing into strips.
4. In a large salad bowl, combine the chopped romaine lettuce, cherry tomatoes, red onion, black beans, corn, diced avocado, shredded cheddar cheese, and fresh cilantro.
5. Add the grilled chicken strips to the salad.
6. Squeeze the lime juice over the salad and season with salt and pepper to taste.
7. Toss the salad gently to mix all ingredients well.
8. Serve immediately with optional toppings like sour cream, salsa, or crushed tortilla chips for added flavor and texture.

Nutritional Values (per serving, based on 4 servings):

- Calories: 350
- Fat: 20g
- Carbohydrates: 18g
- Fiber: 8g
- Protein: 28g

Asian Chicken Lettuce Wraps

Ingredients:

- 1 pound ground chicken
- 2 tablespoons olive oil
- 1 small onion, finely chopped
- 2 cloves garlic, minced

63

- 1 tablespoon fresh ginger, grated
- 1 red bell pepper, finely chopped
- 1/4 cup hoisin sauce
- 2 tablespoons soy sauce (or tamari for gluten-free)
- 1 tablespoon rice vinegar
- 1 teaspoon sesame oil
- 1/4 cup water chestnuts, chopped
- 1/4 cup green onions, chopped
- 1/4 cup fresh cilantro, chopped
- 1 head of butter lettuce or iceberg lettuce, leaves separated
- Optional toppings: shredded carrots, sesame seeds, or sriracha

Directions:

1. In a large skillet, heat the olive oil over medium-high heat. Add the finely chopped onion and cook until softened, about 5 minutes.
2. Add the minced garlic and grated ginger to the skillet, and cook for another minute until fragrant.
3. Add the ground chicken to the skillet, breaking it up with a spoon. Cook until browned and cooked through, about 7-10 minutes.
4. Stir in the finely chopped red bell pepper and cook for an additional 2-3 minutes.
5. In a small bowl, whisk together the hoisin sauce, soy sauce, rice vinegar, and sesame oil. Pour the sauce over the chicken mixture and stir well to combine.
6. Add the chopped water chestnuts and cook for another 2-3 minutes until heated through.
7. Remove the skillet from heat and stir in the chopped green onions and cilantro.
8. To assemble the wraps, spoon a portion of the chicken mixture onto the center of each lettuce leaf.

9. Add optional toppings like shredded carrots, sesame seeds, or a drizzle of sriracha for extra flavor.
10. Serve immediately, allowing everyone to wrap their lettuce leaves around the chicken filling.

Nutritional Values (per serving, based on 4 servings):

- Calories: 290
- Fat: 16g
- Carbohydrates: 14g
- Fiber: 2g
- Protein: 24g

Cucumber and Hummus Sandwiches

Ingredients:

- 4 slices of whole grain bread or low-carb bread, toasted
- 1 cup hummus (store-bought or homemade)
- 1 large cucumber, thinly sliced
- 1/4 red onion, thinly sliced
- 1/4 cup fresh dill, chopped
- Salt and pepper to taste
- Optional: lettuce leaves or spinach for extra greens

Directions:

1. Spread a generous layer of hummus on each slice of toasted bread.
2. Arrange the cucumber slices evenly over two of the hummus-covered bread slices.
3. Top the cucumber slices with thinly sliced red onion.

64

4. Sprinkle the chopped fresh dill over the onions, and season with salt and pepper to taste.
5. If using, add lettuce leaves or spinach on top of the onions for extra greens.
6. Place the remaining two slices of bread on top to form sandwiches.
7. Cut each sandwich in half and serve immediately.

Nutritional Values (per serving, based on 2 servings):

- Calories: 250
- Fat: 12g
- Carbohydrates: 30g (Net carbs may vary based on the type of bread used)
- Fiber: 8g
- Protein: 8g

Lentil and Veggie Bowl

Ingredients:

- 1 cup dried green or brown lentils, rinsed and drained
- 3 cups water or vegetable broth
- 1 tablespoon olive oil
- 1 small onion, finely chopped
- 2 cloves garlic, minced
- 1 red bell pepper, diced
- 1 zucchini, diced
- 1 cup cherry tomatoes, halved
- 1 cup spinach leaves, roughly chopped
- 1 teaspoon ground cumin
- 1/2 teaspoon paprika
- 1/2 teaspoon turmeric
- Salt and pepper to taste
- 1/4 cup fresh parsley, chopped
- Juice of 1 lemon

Directions:

1. In a medium saucepan, combine the rinsed lentils and water or vegetable broth. Bring to a boil, then reduce the heat and let simmer for about 20-25 minutes, or until the lentils are tender but not mushy. Drain any excess liquid and set the lentils aside.
2. In a large skillet, heat the olive oil over medium heat. Add the finely chopped onion and cook until softened, about 5 minutes.
3. Add the minced garlic to the skillet and cook for another minute until fragrant.
4. Stir in the diced red bell pepper and zucchini. Cook for about 5-7 minutes, or until the vegetables are tender.
5. Add the cherry tomatoes and spinach to the skillet, cooking for another 2-3 minutes until the spinach is wilted and the tomatoes are slightly softened.
6. Stir in the cooked lentils, ground cumin, paprika, turmeric, salt, and pepper. Cook for an additional 2-3 minutes to allow the flavors to meld together.
7. Remove the skillet from heat and stir in the chopped fresh parsley and lemon juice.
8. Serve the lentil and veggie mixture in bowls, garnished with additional parsley if desired.

Nutritional Values (per serving, based on 4 servings):

- Calories: 250
- Fat: 6g
- Carbohydrates: 38g
- Fiber: 15g
- Protein: 12g

Keto Chicken Salad

Ingredients:

- 2 cups cooked chicken breast, shredded or diced
- 1/2 cup mayonnaise
- 1 tablespoon Dijon mustard
- 1 tablespoon lemon juice
- 1 celery stalk, finely chopped
- 1/4 cup red onion, finely chopped
- 1/4 cup dill pickles, finely chopped
- 1/4 cup fresh parsley, chopped
- Salt and pepper to taste
- Optional: mixed greens or lettuce leaves for serving

Directions:

1. In a large mixing bowl, combine the shredded or diced cooked chicken breast, mayonnaise, Dijon mustard, and lemon juice. Mix until well combined.
2. Add the finely chopped celery, red onion, dill pickles, and fresh parsley to the bowl. Stir to incorporate all the ingredients evenly.
3. Season the chicken salad with salt and pepper to taste.
4. Serve the keto chicken salad on its own, or over a bed of mixed greens or lettuce leaves for a refreshing low-carb meal.
5. Store any leftovers in an airtight container in the refrigerator for up to 3 days.

Nutritional Values (per serving, based on 4 servings):

- Calories: 250
- Fat: 20g
- Carbohydrates: 2g
- Fiber: 1g
- Protein: 18g

Greek Yogurt Chicken Salad

Ingredients:

- 2 cups cooked chicken breast, shredded or diced
- 1/2 cup Greek yogurt (plain, unsweetened)
- 1 tablespoon Dijon mustard
- 1 tablespoon lemon juice
- 1 celery stalk, finely chopped
- 1/4 cup red onion, finely chopped
- 1/4 cup red grapes, halved (optional)
- 1/4 cup chopped walnuts or almonds (optional)
- 1/4 cup fresh parsley, chopped
- Salt and pepper to taste
- Optional: mixed greens or lettuce leaves for serving

Directions:

1. In a large mixing bowl, combine the shredded or diced cooked chicken breast, Greek yogurt, Dijon mustard, and lemon juice. Mix until well combined.
2. Add the finely chopped celery, red onion, and fresh parsley to the bowl. Stir to incorporate all the ingredients evenly.
3. If using, gently fold in the halved red grapes and chopped nuts for added flavor and texture.
4. Season the chicken salad with salt and pepper to taste.
5. Serve the Greek yogurt chicken salad on its own, or over a bed of mixed greens or lettuce leaves for a refreshing and healthy meal.

6. Store any leftovers in an airtight container in the refrigerator for up to 3 days.

Nutritional Values (per serving, based on 4 servings):

- Calories: 210
- Fat: 8g
- Carbohydrates: 6g
- Fiber: 1g
- Protein: 28g

Stuffed Bell Peppers

Ingredients:

- 4 large bell peppers (any color)
- 1 pound ground beef (or turkey or chicken)
- 1 small onion, finely chopped
- 2 cloves garlic, minced
- 1 cup cooked quinoa (or brown rice or cauliflower rice)
- 1 cup marinara sauce (sugar-free)
- 1 teaspoon dried oregano
- 1 teaspoon dried basil
- 1/2 teaspoon salt
- 1/2 teaspoon black pepper
- 1 cup shredded mozzarella cheese
- 1/4 cup grated Parmesan cheese
- Fresh parsley, chopped, for garnish

Directions:

1. Preheat your oven to 375°F (190°C).
2. Cut the tops off the bell peppers and remove the seeds and membranes. If necessary, trim the bottoms slightly so the peppers stand upright. Place the peppers in a baking dish.
3. In a large skillet, heat a small amount of olive oil over medium heat. Add the finely chopped onion and cook until softened, about 5 minutes.
4. Add the minced garlic to the skillet and cook for another minute until fragrant.
5. Add the ground beef to the skillet and cook until browned, breaking it up with a spoon as it cooks. Drain any excess fat.
6. Stir in the cooked quinoa, marinara sauce, dried oregano, dried basil, salt, and black pepper. Cook for a few more minutes until everything is well combined and heated through.
7. Remove the skillet from heat and stir in half of the shredded mozzarella cheese.
8. Spoon the beef and quinoa mixture evenly into the hollowed bell peppers.
9. Top each stuffed pepper with the remaining shredded mozzarella cheese and grated Parmesan cheese.
10. Cover the baking dish with foil and bake in the preheated oven for 30 minutes.
11. Remove the foil and bake for an additional 10-15 minutes, or until the cheese is melted and bubbly and the peppers are tender.
12. Remove from the oven and let cool for a few minutes before serving.
13. Garnish with chopped fresh parsley and serve.

Nutritional Values (per serving, based on 4 servings):

- Calories: 350
- Fat: 18g
- Carbohydrates: 20g
- Fiber: 4g
- Protein: 28g

Cobb Salad

Ingredients:

- 6 cups romaine lettuce, chopped
- 2 cups cooked chicken breast, diced
- 4 hard-boiled eggs, peeled and quartered
- 1 large avocado, diced
- 1 cup cherry tomatoes, halved
- 1/2 cup blue cheese, crumbled
- 4 slices cooked bacon, crumbled
- 1/4 cup red onion, thinly sliced
- 1/4 cup fresh chives, chopped

Dressing:

- 1/4 cup red wine vinegar
- 1/2 cup olive oil
- 1 tablespoon Dijon mustard
- 1 teaspoon Worcestershire sauce
- Salt and pepper to taste

Directions:

1. In a large salad bowl, arrange the chopped romaine lettuce as the base.
2. Arrange the diced chicken, hard-boiled eggs, avocado, cherry tomatoes, crumbled blue cheese, crumbled bacon, and sliced red onion in rows on top of the lettuce.
3. In a small bowl, whisk together the red wine vinegar, olive oil, Dijon mustard, Worcestershire sauce, salt, and pepper until well combined.
4. Drizzle the dressing over the salad just before serving, or serve the dressing on the side.
5. Garnish the salad with chopped fresh chives.
6. Toss gently to combine all the ingredients or leave it arranged for a more aesthetic presentation.

Nutritional Values (per serving, based on 4 servings):

- Calories: 450
- Fat: 35g
- Carbohydrates: 10g
- Fiber: 5g
- Protein: 25g

Chicken and Asparagus Lemon Stir Fry

Ingredients:

- 6 cups romaine lettuce, chopped
- 2 cups cooked chicken breast, diced
- 4 hard-boiled eggs, peeled and quartered
- 1 large avocado, diced
- 1 cup cherry tomatoes, halved
- 1/2 cup blue cheese, crumbled
- 4 slices cooked bacon, crumbled
- 1/4 cup red onion, thinly sliced
- 1/4 cup fresh chives, chopped

Dressing:

- 1/4 cup red wine vinegar
- 1/2 cup olive oil
- 1 tablespoon Dijon mustard
- 1 teaspoon Worcestershire sauce
- Salt and pepper to taste

Directions:

1. In a large salad bowl, arrange the chopped romaine lettuce as the base.
2. Arrange the diced chicken, hard-boiled eggs, avocado, cherry tomatoes, crumbled blue cheese, crumbled bacon, and sliced red onion in rows on top of the lettuce.

3. In a small bowl, whisk together the red wine vinegar, olive oil, Dijon mustard, Worcestershire sauce, salt, and pepper until well combined.
4. Drizzle the dressing over the salad just before serving, or serve the dressing on the side.
5. Garnish the salad with chopped fresh chives.
6. Toss gently to combine all the ingredients or leave it arranged for a more aesthetic presentation.

Nutritional Values (per serving, based on 4 servings):

- Calories: 450
- Fat: 35g
- Carbohydrates: 10g
- Fiber: 5g
- Protein: 25g

Cream of Mushroom Soup

Ingredients:

- 2 tablespoons butter
- 1 tablespoon olive oil
- 1 large onion, finely chopped
- 3 cloves garlic, minced
- 1 pound mixed mushrooms (such as cremini, shiitake, and white button), sliced
- 1 teaspoon dried thyme
- 4 cups low-sodium chicken or vegetable broth
- 1 cup heavy cream
- 1/4 cup all-purpose flour (or gluten-free flour)
- 1/2 cup dry white wine (optional)
- Salt and pepper to taste
- Fresh parsley, chopped, for garnish

Directions:

1. In a large pot, heat the butter and olive oil over medium heat until the butter is melted.
2. Add the finely chopped onion and cook until softened, about 5 minutes.
3. Add the minced garlic and cook for another minute until fragrant.
4. Add the sliced mushrooms and cook until they release their moisture and begin to brown, about 10 minutes.
5. Sprinkle the flour over the mushrooms and stir well to coat. Cook for another 2 minutes to eliminate the raw flour taste.
6. Slowly pour in the white wine (if using) and cook for a few minutes until the liquid is mostly evaporated.
7. Add the dried thyme and low-sodium broth to the pot. Bring to a simmer and cook for about 15 minutes, allowing the flavors to meld.
8. Using an immersion blender, blend the soup until smooth. Alternatively, you can transfer the soup in batches to a blender and blend until smooth. Return the blended soup to the pot.
9. Stir in the heavy cream and season with salt and pepper to taste. Cook for another 5 minutes until heated through.
10. Serve the soup hot, garnished with chopped fresh parsley.

Nutritional Values (per serving, based on 4 servings):

- Calories: 300
- Fat: 24g
- Carbohydrates: 16g
- Fiber: 2g
- Protein: 7g

SCAN THE QR CODE AND IMMEDIATELY ACCESS YOUR 3 SPECIAL BONUSES IN DIGITAL FORMAT!

CHAPTER 3
DELICIOUS DINNERS

This chapter is designed to provide you with a variety of hearty, flavorful recipes that make the perfect end to your day. Whether you're looking for something quick and easy or a dish that's a bit more indulgent, you'll find a range of options to suit every taste and dietary need. From comforting classics to innovative new dishes, each recipe is crafted to deliver maximum flavor while supporting your health goals. Get ready to transform your evening meals into a delicious experience with these mouthwatering dinner recipes.

Baked Salmon with Dill Sauce

Ingredients:

- 4 salmon fillets (about 6 ounces each)
- 2 tablespoons olive oil
- Salt and pepper to taste
- 1 lemon, thinly sliced

Dill Sauce:

- 1/2 cup Greek yogurt (plain, unsweetened)
- 2 tablespoons fresh dill, chopped
- 1 tablespoon lemon juice
- 1 teaspoon Dijon mustard
- 1 clove garlic, minced
- Salt and pepper to taste

Directions:

1. Preheat your oven to 375°F (190°C). Line a baking sheet with parchment paper.
2. Place the salmon fillets on the prepared baking sheet. Drizzle them with olive oil and season with salt and pepper. Arrange lemon slices on top of each fillet.
3. Bake the salmon in the preheated oven for 15-20 minutes, or until the salmon is opaque and flakes easily with a fork.
4. While the salmon is baking, prepare the dill sauce. In a small bowl, combine the Greek yogurt, chopped fresh dill, lemon juice, Dijon mustard, minced garlic, salt, and pepper. Mix until well combined.
5. Remove the salmon from the oven and let it rest for a few minutes.
6. Serve the baked salmon fillets with a generous dollop of dill sauce on top or on the side.

Nutritional Values (per serving, based on 4 servings):

- Calories: 350
- Fat: 22g
- Carbohydrates: 3g
- Fiber: 1g
- Protein: 35g

Roast Chicken with Herbs

Ingredients:

- 1 whole chicken (about 4-5 pounds)
- 3 tablespoons olive oil
- 2 tablespoons fresh rosemary, chopped

- 2 tablespoons fresh thyme, chopped
- 2 tablespoons fresh parsley, chopped
- 4 cloves garlic, minced
- 1 lemon, halved
- Salt and pepper to taste
- 1 onion, quartered
- 2 carrots, cut into large chunks
- 2 celery stalks, cut into large chunks

Directions:

1. Preheat your oven to 375°F (190°C).
2. In a small bowl, combine the olive oil, chopped rosemary, thyme, parsley, minced garlic, salt, and pepper. Mix well to create a herb paste.
3. Pat the chicken dry with paper towels. Rub the herb paste all over the chicken, including under the skin and inside the cavity.
4. Squeeze the juice of one lemon half over the chicken and place both lemon halves inside the cavity.
5. Arrange the onion, carrots, and celery around the chicken in a roasting pan.
6. Roast the chicken in the preheated oven for about 1 hour and 30 minutes, or until the internal temperature reaches 165°F (74°C) and the juices run clear. Baste the chicken with its juices halfway through cooking.
7. Remove the chicken from the oven and let it rest for 10-15 minutes before carving.
8. Serve the roast chicken with the roasted vegetables on the side.

Nutritional Values (per serving, based on 6 servings):

- Calories: 400
- Fat: 25g
- Carbohydrates: 6g
- Fiber: 2g
- Protein: 35g

Grilled Steak with Garlic Butter

Ingredients:

- 4 ribeye or sirloin steaks (about 1-inch thick)
- 2 tablespoons olive oil
- Salt and pepper to taste
- 4 tablespoons unsalted butter, softened
- 3 cloves garlic, minced
- 2 tablespoons fresh parsley, chopped
- 1 tablespoon fresh rosemary, chopped
- 1 tablespoon fresh thyme, chopped

Directions:

1. Preheat your grill to medium-high heat.
2. Rub the steaks with olive oil and season generously with salt and pepper on both sides.
3. In a small bowl, combine the softened butter, minced garlic, chopped parsley, rosemary, and thyme. Mix well to create the garlic herb butter.
4. Grill the steaks for about 4-5 minutes on each side for medium-rare, or until they reach your desired level of doneness. Use a meat thermometer to check the internal temperature (130°F for medium-rare, 140°F for medium).
5. Remove the steaks from the grill and place a dollop of the garlic herb butter on each steak while they are still hot. Let the steaks rest for about 5 minutes, allowing the butter to melt and the juices to redistribute.
6. Serve the grilled steaks hot, topped with the melted garlic herb butter.

Nutritional Values (per serving, based on 4 servings):

- Calories: 520
- Fat: 40g
- Carbohydrates: 2g
- Fiber: 0g
- Protein: 38g

Pork Tenderloin with Roasted Brussels Sprouts

Ingredients:

- 1.5 pounds pork tenderloin
- 2 tablespoons olive oil
- 2 tablespoons Dijon mustard
- 1 tablespoon honey
- 3 cloves garlic, minced
- 1 teaspoon dried thyme
- Salt and pepper to taste
- 1 pound Brussels sprouts, trimmed and halved
- 1 tablespoon balsamic vinegar

Directions:

1. Preheat your oven to 400°F (200°C). Line a baking sheet with parchment paper or foil.
2. In a small bowl, mix together 1 tablespoon of olive oil, Dijon mustard, honey, minced garlic, dried thyme, salt, and pepper. Rub this mixture all over the pork tenderloin.
3. In another bowl, toss the halved Brussels sprouts with the remaining 1 tablespoon of olive oil, balsamic vinegar, salt, and pepper.
4. Place the pork tenderloin in the center of the prepared baking sheet and arrange the Brussels sprouts around it in a single layer.
5. Roast in the preheated oven for about 25-30 minutes, or until the internal temperature of the pork reaches 145°F (63°C) and the Brussels sprouts are tender and caramelized. Stir the Brussels sprouts halfway through roasting to ensure even cooking.
6. Remove the baking sheet from the oven and let the pork tenderloin rest for 5-10 minutes before slicing.
7. Slice the pork tenderloin into medallions and serve with the roasted Brussels sprouts.

Nutritional Values (per serving, based on 4 servings):

- Calories: 350
- Fat: 15g
- Carbohydrates: 15g
- Fiber: 4g
- Protein: 40g

Spaghetti Squash with Marinara Sauce

Ingredients:

- 1 large spaghetti squash
- 2 tablespoons olive oil
- Salt and pepper to taste
- 1 jar (24 oz) marinara sauce (sugar-free preferred)
- 1/2 teaspoon dried oregano
- 1/2 teaspoon dried basil
- 2 cloves garlic, minced
- 1/4 cup grated Parmesan cheese
- Fresh basil, chopped, for garnish

Directions:

1. Preheat your oven to 400°F (200°C). Line a baking sheet with parchment paper or foil.
2. Cut the spaghetti squash in half lengthwise and scoop out the seeds. Drizzle the inside of each half with olive oil and season with salt and pepper.
3. Place the squash halves cut-side down on the prepared baking sheet. Roast in the preheated oven for about 40-45 minutes, or until the flesh is tender and can be easily shredded with a fork.
4. While the squash is roasting, heat a saucepan over medium heat. Add a small amount of olive oil and the minced garlic, cooking until fragrant, about 1 minute.
5. Add the marinara sauce, dried oregano, and dried basil to the saucepan. Stir well to combine and let it simmer on low heat for about 10-15 minutes, allowing the flavors to meld.
6. Once the spaghetti squash is done roasting, remove it from the oven and let it cool for a few minutes. Use a fork to scrape out the flesh into long, spaghetti-like strands.
7. Divide the spaghetti squash strands among serving plates and top with the marinara sauce.
8. Sprinkle with grated Parmesan cheese and garnish with chopped fresh basil.
9. Serve immediately and enjoy.

Nutritional Values (per serving, based on 4 servings):

- Calories: 180
- Fat: 8g
- Carbohydrates: 22g
- Fiber: 6g
- Protein: 5g

Baked Trout with Lemon and Herbs

Ingredients:

- 4 trout fillets
- 2 tablespoons olive oil
- 2 lemons, thinly sliced
- 3 cloves garlic, minced
- 2 tablespoons fresh parsley, chopped
- 1 tablespoon fresh dill, chopped
- 1 tablespoon fresh thyme, chopped
- Salt and pepper to taste
- Lemon wedges, for serving

Directions:

1. Preheat your oven to 375°F (190°C). Line a baking sheet with parchment paper or foil.
2. Place the trout fillets on the prepared baking sheet. Drizzle with olive oil and season with salt and pepper.
3. Arrange lemon slices over the trout fillets.
4. In a small bowl, combine the minced garlic, fresh parsley, dill, and thyme. Sprinkle the herb mixture evenly over the trout fillets.
5. Bake in the preheated oven for 15-20 minutes, or until the trout is opaque and flakes easily with a fork.
6. Remove the trout from the oven and let it rest for a few minutes.
7. Serve the baked trout fillets with additional lemon wedges on the side for squeezing over the top.

Nutritional Values (per serving, based on 4 servings):

- Calories: 280

- Fat: 16g
- Carbohydrates: 4g
- Fiber: 1g
- Protein: 30g

Vegan Chili

Ingredients:

- 2 tablespoons olive oil
- 1 large onion, chopped
- 3 cloves garlic, minced
- 1 red bell pepper, diced
- 1 yellow bell pepper, diced
- 1 zucchini, diced
- 2 carrots, peeled and diced
- 1 cup corn kernels (fresh or frozen)
- 2 cans (15 oz each) black beans, drained and rinsed
- 1 can (15 oz) kidney beans, drained and rinsed
- 1 can (28 oz) diced tomatoes
- 1 can (15 oz) tomato sauce
- 2 tablespoons chili powder
- 1 teaspoon ground cumin
- 1 teaspoon smoked paprika
- 1/2 teaspoon ground coriander
- 1/2 teaspoon cayenne pepper (optional, for heat)
- Salt and pepper to taste
- 1 cup vegetable broth
- 1/4 cup fresh cilantro, chopped (for garnish)
- Optional toppings: avocado slices, vegan sour cream, green onions, or tortilla chips

Directions:

1. In a large pot or Dutch oven, heat the olive oil over medium heat. Add the chopped onion and cook until softened, about 5 minutes.
2. Add the minced garlic, diced red and yellow bell peppers, zucchini, and carrots to the pot. Cook for another 5-7 minutes, stirring occasionally, until the vegetables begin to soften.
3. Stir in the corn kernels, black beans, kidney beans, diced tomatoes (with their juice), tomato sauce, chili powder, ground cumin, smoked paprika, ground coriander, cayenne pepper (if using), salt, and pepper.
4. Pour in the vegetable broth and stir well to combine all the ingredients.
5. Bring the chili to a boil, then reduce the heat to low and let it simmer for about 30-40 minutes, or until the vegetables are tender and the flavors have melded together. Stir occasionally.
6. Taste and adjust seasoning if needed.
7. Serve the vegan chili hot, garnished with fresh cilantro and your choice of optional toppings like avocado slices, vegan sour cream, green onions, or tortilla chips.

Nutritional Values (per serving, based on 6 servings):

- Calories: 250
- Fat: 7g
- Carbohydrates: 38g
- Fiber: 12g
- Protein: 10g

Slow Cooker Beef Stew

Ingredients:

- 2 pounds beef chuck roast, cut into 1-inch cubes

- 3 tablespoons all-purpose flour (or gluten-free flour)
- Salt and pepper to taste
- 2 tablespoons olive oil
- 4 cups beef broth
- 1 cup red wine (optional)
- 2 tablespoons tomato paste
- 1 tablespoon Worcestershire sauce
- 4 cloves garlic, minced
- 1 large onion, chopped
- 3 carrots, peeled and sliced
- 3 celery stalks, sliced
- 4 large potatoes, peeled and diced
- 2 bay leaves
- 1 teaspoon dried thyme
- 1 teaspoon dried rosemary
- 1 cup frozen peas
- Fresh parsley, chopped, for garnish

Directions:

1. In a large bowl, toss the beef cubes with the flour, salt, and pepper until evenly coated.
2. Heat the olive oil in a large skillet over medium-high heat. Add the beef cubes and brown on all sides, about 5-7 minutes. You may need to do this in batches to avoid overcrowding the skillet.
3. Transfer the browned beef to a slow cooker.
4. Add the beef broth, red wine (if using), tomato paste, Worcestershire sauce, minced garlic, chopped onion, carrots, celery, potatoes, bay leaves, thyme, and rosemary to the slow cooker. Stir well to combine.
5. Cover and cook on low for 7-8 hours, or on high for 4-5 hours, until the beef is tender and the vegetables are cooked through.

6. About 30 minutes before the stew is done, stir in the frozen peas.
7. Remove the bay leaves and discard them.
8. Taste and adjust seasoning with additional salt and pepper if needed.
9. Serve the beef stew hot, garnished with chopped fresh parsley.

Nutritional Values (per serving, based on 6 servings):

- Calories: 400
- Fat: 18g
- Carbohydrates: 32g
- Fiber: 6g
- Protein: 28g

Baked Garlic Parmesan Chicken

Ingredients:

- 4 boneless, skinless chicken breasts
- 1/2 cup grated Parmesan cheese
- 1/4 cup breadcrumbs (or almond flour for a low-carb option)
- 2 tablespoons fresh parsley, chopped
- 4 cloves garlic, minced
- 1 teaspoon dried oregano
- 1 teaspoon dried basil
- 1/2 teaspoon salt
- 1/4 teaspoon black pepper
- 1/4 cup unsalted butter, melted
- Lemon wedges, for serving

Directions:

1. Preheat your oven to 375°F (190°C). Line a baking sheet with parchment paper or lightly grease a baking dish.
2. In a small bowl, combine the grated Parmesan cheese, breadcrumbs (or almond flour), chopped parsley, minced

garlic, dried oregano, dried basil, salt, and black pepper.

3. Dip each chicken breast into the melted butter, coating both sides.

4. Press the chicken breasts into the Parmesan mixture, ensuring they are well-coated on both sides.

5. Place the coated chicken breasts on the prepared baking sheet or in the baking dish.

6. Drizzle any remaining melted butter over the top of the chicken.

7. Bake in the preheated oven for 25-30 minutes, or until the chicken is cooked through and reaches an internal temperature of 165°F (74°C). The coating should be golden brown and crispy.

8. Remove the chicken from the oven and let it rest for a few minutes before serving.

9. Serve the baked garlic Parmesan chicken with lemon wedges on the side for squeezing over the top.

Nutritional Values (per serving, based on 4 servings):

- Calories: 350
- Fat: 20g
- Carbohydrates: 4g
- Fiber: 1g
- Protein: 35g

Stuffed Eggplant

Ingredients:

- 2 large eggplants
- 2 tablespoons olive oil
- 1 pound ground beef (or ground turkey)
- 1 small onion, finely chopped
- 3 cloves garlic, minced
- 1 red bell pepper, diced
- 1 can (15 oz) diced tomatoes, drained
- 1 teaspoon dried oregano
- 1 teaspoon dried basil
- 1/2 teaspoon salt
- 1/4 teaspoon black pepper
- 1/2 cup grated Parmesan cheese
- 1 cup shredded mozzarella cheese
- Fresh parsley, chopped, for garnish

Directions:

1. Preheat your oven to 375°F (190°C). Line a baking sheet with parchment paper or lightly grease a baking dish.

2. Cut the eggplants in half lengthwise. Scoop out the flesh, leaving about 1/2-inch border around the edges to create a shell. Chop the scooped-out flesh and set aside.

3. Place the eggplant shells on the prepared baking sheet, brush with 1 tablespoon of olive oil, and season with a pinch of salt and pepper. Bake in the preheated oven for about 15 minutes, or until they start to soften.

4. While the eggplant shells are baking, heat the remaining 1 tablespoon of olive oil in a large skillet over medium heat. Add the finely chopped onion and cook until softened, about 5 minutes.

5. Add the minced garlic and cook for another minute until fragrant.

6. Add the ground beef to the skillet and cook until browned, breaking it up with a spoon as it cooks. Drain any excess fat.

7. Stir in the diced red bell pepper and the chopped eggplant flesh. Cook for another 5 minutes until the vegetables are tender.

8. Add the drained diced tomatoes, dried oregano, dried basil, salt, and black pepper to the skillet. Cook for another 3-4 minutes, allowing the flavors to meld.

9. Remove the skillet from heat and stir in the grated Parmesan cheese.

10. Spoon the beef and vegetable mixture evenly into the eggplant shells.

11. Sprinkle the shredded mozzarella cheese over the top of the stuffed eggplants.

12. Return the eggplants to the oven and bake for another 20-25 minutes, or until the cheese is melted and bubbly, and the eggplants are tender.

13. Remove from the oven and let cool for a few minutes before serving.

14. Garnish with chopped fresh parsley and serve.

Nutritional Values (per serving, based on 4 servings):

- Calories: 350
- Fat: 22g
- Carbohydrates: 15g
- Fiber: 6g
- Protein: 25g

Turkey Meatballs with Zucchini Noodles

Ingredients:

- 1 pound ground turkey
- 1/4 cup almond flour (or breadcrumbs)
- 1/4 cup grated Parmesan cheese
- 1 large egg
- 2 cloves garlic, minced
- 1 tablespoon fresh parsley, chopped
- 1 teaspoon dried oregano
- 1/2 teaspoon salt
- 1/4 teaspoon black pepper
- 2 tablespoons olive oil
- 1 jar (24 oz) marinara sauce (sugar-free preferred)
- 4 medium zucchini, spiralized into noodles
- Fresh basil, chopped, for garnish

Directions:

1. In a large bowl, combine the ground turkey, almond flour (or breadcrumbs), grated Parmesan cheese, egg, minced garlic, chopped parsley, dried oregano, salt, and black pepper. Mix well until all ingredients are evenly incorporated.

2. Form the mixture into small meatballs, about 1-inch in diameter, and set them aside on a plate.

3. Heat 1 tablespoon of olive oil in a large skillet over medium-high heat. Add the meatballs in batches, being careful not to overcrowd the pan. Cook for about 5-7 minutes, turning occasionally, until the meatballs are browned on all sides and cooked through. Remove the meatballs from the skillet and set them aside.

4. In the same skillet, add the marinara sauce and bring it to a simmer over medium heat. Return the meatballs to the skillet and let them simmer in the sauce for about 10 minutes, allowing the flavors to meld.

5. While the meatballs are simmering, heat the remaining 1 tablespoon of olive oil in another large skillet over medium heat. Add the spiralized zucchini noodles and cook for about 3-4 minutes, tossing gently, until they are tender but still slightly crisp.

6. To serve, divide the zucchini noodles among serving plates and top with the turkey meatballs and marinara sauce.

7. Garnish with chopped fresh basil and additional grated Parmesan cheese if desired.

Nutritional Values (per serving, based on 4 servings):

- Calories: 300
- Fat: 18g
- Carbohydrates: 10g
- Fiber: 4g
- Protein: 25g

Pan-Seared Tilapia with Lemon Butter Sauce

Ingredients:

- 4 tilapia fillets
- Salt and pepper to taste
- 2 tablespoons olive oil
- 1/4 cup all-purpose flour (or almond flour for a low-carb option)
- 1/4 cup unsalted butter
- 3 cloves garlic, minced
- 1/4 cup fresh lemon juice (about 2 lemons)
- 1/4 cup chicken broth
- 2 tablespoons fresh parsley, chopped
- Lemon slices, for garnish

Directions:

1. Pat the tilapia fillets dry with paper towels and season both sides with salt and pepper.
2. Lightly coat each fillet with flour, shaking off any excess.
3. Heat the olive oil in a large skillet over medium-high heat. Add the tilapia fillets to the skillet and cook for 3-4 minutes on each side, or until golden brown and cooked through. Transfer the cooked fillets to a plate and cover with foil to keep warm.
4. In the same skillet, reduce the heat to medium and add the butter. Once the butter is melted, add the minced garlic and cook for about 1 minute until fragrant.
5. Pour in the fresh lemon juice and chicken broth, stirring to combine. Let the sauce simmer for 2-3 minutes, allowing it to reduce slightly.
6. Stir in the chopped fresh parsley.
7. Return the tilapia fillets to the skillet, spooning some of the lemon butter sauce over the top. Cook for another 1-2 minutes until the fish is heated through.
8. Serve the pan-seared tilapia with lemon butter sauce, garnished with lemon slices and additional fresh parsley if desired.

Nutritional Values (per serving, based on 4 servings):

- Calories: 320
- Fat: 20g
- Carbohydrates: 6g
- Fiber: 1g
- Protein: 28g

Vegetarian Stir Fry with Tofu

Ingredients:

- 1 block (14 oz) firm tofu, drained and pressed
- 2 tablespoons soy sauce (or tamari for gluten-free)
- 1 tablespoon sesame oil
- 2 tablespoons olive oil
- 1 red bell pepper, sliced
- 1 yellow bell pepper, sliced
- 1 cup broccoli florets

- 1 cup snap peas
- 1 carrot, julienned
- 2 cloves garlic, minced
- 1 tablespoon fresh ginger, grated
- 1/4 cup vegetable broth
- 2 tablespoons hoisin sauce
- 1 tablespoon rice vinegar
- 1 tablespoon cornstarch mixed with 2 tablespoons water
- 2 green onions, sliced
- 1 tablespoon sesame seeds
- Cooked rice or noodles, for serving

Directions:

1. Cut the pressed tofu into 1-inch cubes. In a bowl, toss the tofu cubes with soy sauce and sesame oil. Let it marinate for at least 15 minutes.
2. Heat 1 tablespoon of olive oil in a large skillet or wok over medium-high heat. Add the marinated tofu and cook until golden brown on all sides, about 5-7 minutes. Remove the tofu from the skillet and set aside.
3. In the same skillet, add the remaining 1 tablespoon of olive oil. Add the sliced red and yellow bell peppers, broccoli florets, snap peas, and julienned carrot. Stir-fry for about 5 minutes, or until the vegetables are tender-crisp.
4. Add the minced garlic and grated ginger to the skillet, and cook for another minute until fragrant.
5. In a small bowl, whisk together the vegetable broth, hoisin sauce, and rice vinegar. Pour the sauce into the skillet and stir to combine with the vegetables.
6. Return the tofu to the skillet, and toss to coat it with the sauce.

7. Pour the cornstarch mixture into the skillet, stirring constantly until the sauce thickens, about 2-3 minutes.
8. Remove the skillet from heat and stir in the sliced green onions and sesame seeds.
9. Serve the vegetarian stir fry with tofu over cooked rice or noodles.

Nutritional Values (per serving, based on 4 servings):

- Calories: 280
- Fat: 18g
- Carbohydrates: 20g
- Fiber: 5g
- Protein: 12g

Lamb Chops with Mint Pesto

Ingredients:

- 8 lamb chops, about 1-inch thick
- 2 tablespoons olive oil
- Salt and pepper to taste
- 2 cloves garlic, minced
- 1 tablespoon fresh rosemary, chopped

Mint Pesto:

- 1 cup fresh mint leaves
- 1/2 cup fresh parsley leaves
- 1/4 cup pine nuts or walnuts
- 1/2 cup grated Parmesan cheese
- 2 cloves garlic
- 1/2 cup olive oil
- Salt and pepper to taste
- Juice of 1 lemon

Directions:

1. In a small bowl, combine the minced garlic, chopped rosemary, olive oil, salt, and pepper. Rub this mixture all over the

lamb chops and let them marinate for at least 30 minutes at room temperature.

2. While the lamb chops are marinating, prepare the mint pesto. In a food processor, combine the fresh mint leaves, parsley leaves, pine nuts (or walnuts), grated Parmesan cheese, and garlic. Pulse until the ingredients are finely chopped.

3. With the food processor running, slowly drizzle in the olive oil until the pesto reaches your desired consistency. Season with salt, pepper, and lemon juice to taste. Set aside.

4. Preheat your grill or a grill pan over medium-high heat. Grill the lamb chops for about 4-5 minutes on each side for medium-rare, or until they reach your desired level of doneness. Use a meat thermometer to check the internal temperature (130°F for medium-rare, 140°F for medium).

5. Remove the lamb chops from the grill and let them rest for a few minutes.

6. Serve the grilled lamb chops hot, topped with a generous spoonful of mint pesto.

Nutritional Values (per serving, based on 4 servings):

- Calories: 450
- Fat: 36g
- Carbohydrates: 4g
- Fiber: 1g
- Protein: 28g

Garlic Shrimp with Spaghetti Squash

Ingredients:

- 1 large spaghetti squash
- 2 tablespoons olive oil
- Salt and pepper to taste
- 1 pound large shrimp, peeled and deveined
- 4 cloves garlic, minced
- 1/4 teaspoon red pepper flakes (optional)
- 1/4 cup chicken broth
- 2 tablespoons lemon juice
- 1/4 cup fresh parsley, chopped
- 1/4 cup grated Parmesan cheese
- Lemon wedges, for serving

Directions:

1. Preheat your oven to 400°F (200°C). Line a baking sheet with parchment paper or foil.

2. Cut the spaghetti squash in half lengthwise and scoop out the seeds. Drizzle the inside of each half with 1 tablespoon of olive oil and season with salt and pepper.

3. Place the squash halves cut-side down on the prepared baking sheet. Roast in the preheated oven for about 40-45 minutes, or until the flesh is tender and can be easily shredded with a fork.

4. While the squash is roasting, heat the remaining 1 tablespoon of olive oil in a large skillet over medium heat. Add the minced garlic and red pepper flakes (if using) and cook for about 1 minute until fragrant.

5. Add the shrimp to the skillet and cook for about 2-3 minutes on each side, or until the shrimp are pink and opaque. Remove the shrimp from the skillet and set aside.

6. In the same skillet, add the chicken broth and lemon juice, stirring to deglaze the pan. Cook for about 2 minutes, allowing the sauce to reduce slightly.

7. Once the spaghetti squash is done roasting, remove it from the oven and let it cool for a few minutes. Use a fork to

scrape out the flesh into long, spaghetti-like strands.

8. Add the spaghetti squash strands to the skillet with the sauce, tossing to coat evenly.

9. Return the cooked shrimp to the skillet and toss to combine with the spaghetti squash and sauce.

10. Remove from heat and stir in the chopped fresh parsley and grated Parmesan cheese.

11. Serve the garlic shrimp with spaghetti squash hot, with lemon wedges on the side for squeezing over the top.

Nutritional Values (per serving, based on 4 servings):

- Calories: 280
- Fat: 12g
- Carbohydrates: 16g
- Fiber: 4g
- Protein: 28g

Low-Carb Shepherd's Pie

Ingredients:

- 1 pound ground beef (or ground lamb)
- 1 small onion, finely chopped
- 2 cloves garlic, minced
- 1 cup carrots, diced
- 1 cup celery, diced
- 1 cup mushrooms, sliced
- 1 cup green beans, chopped
- 1 cup beef broth
- 1 tablespoon tomato paste
- 1 teaspoon Worcestershire sauce
- 1 teaspoon dried thyme
- 1 teaspoon dried rosemary
- Salt and pepper to taste
- 1 large cauliflower head, cut into florets

- 2 tablespoons butter
- 1/4 cup heavy cream
- 1/4 cup grated Parmesan cheese
- Fresh parsley, chopped, for garnish

Directions:

1. Preheat your oven to 375°F (190°C).

2. In a large skillet, cook the ground beef over medium heat until browned. Drain any excess fat.

3. Add the chopped onion and minced garlic to the skillet, cooking until the onion is softened, about 5 minutes.

4. Stir in the diced carrots, celery, mushrooms, and green beans. Cook for another 5-7 minutes, until the vegetables are tender.

5. Add the beef broth, tomato paste, Worcestershire sauce, dried thyme, dried rosemary, salt, and pepper to the skillet. Stir well to combine and let the mixture simmer for about 10 minutes, until the sauce has thickened slightly.

6. While the meat and vegetable mixture is simmering, prepare the cauliflower mash. Steam or boil the cauliflower florets until tender, about 10-15 minutes. Drain well and transfer to a food processor.

7. Add the butter, heavy cream, and grated Parmesan cheese to the cauliflower. Process until smooth and creamy. Season with salt and pepper to taste.

8. Transfer the meat and vegetable mixture to a baking dish, spreading it out evenly.

9. Spoon the cauliflower mash over the top of the meat mixture, spreading it out evenly to cover.

10. Bake in the preheated oven for 20-25 minutes, or until the top is golden and the filling is bubbling.

11. Remove from the oven and let cool for a few minutes before serving.
12. Garnish with chopped fresh parsley and serve.

Nutritional Values (per serving, based on 6 servings):

- Calories: 300
- Fat: 18g
- Carbohydrates: 12g
- Fiber: 4g
- Protein: 20g

Seared Scallops with Cauliflower Puree

Ingredients:

- 1 pound large sea scallops, patted dry
- Salt and pepper to taste
- 2 tablespoons olive oil
- 2 tablespoons butter
- 1 large cauliflower head, cut into florets
- 1/2 cup heavy cream
- 2 cloves garlic, minced
- 1/4 cup grated Parmesan cheese
- 1 tablespoon fresh lemon juice
- Fresh chives, chopped, for garnish

Directions:

1. Begin by preparing the cauliflower puree. Steam or boil the cauliflower florets until tender, about 10-15 minutes. Drain well and transfer to a blender or food processor.
2. Add the heavy cream, minced garlic, and grated Parmesan cheese to the cauliflower. Blend until smooth and creamy. Season with salt and pepper to taste. Keep the puree warm while you prepare the scallops.
3. Season the scallops on both sides with salt and pepper.
4. Heat the olive oil in a large skillet over medium-high heat. When the oil is hot, add the scallops, making sure they are not touching each other. Sear for about 2-3 minutes on each side, or until they develop a golden-brown crust and are cooked through. Do not overcrowd the pan; sear in batches if necessary.
5. Remove the scallops from the skillet and set aside. Add the butter to the same skillet and let it melt, scraping up any browned bits from the bottom of the pan. Stir in the fresh lemon juice.
6. To serve, spread a generous spoonful of cauliflower puree on each plate. Top with seared scallops and drizzle with the lemon butter sauce from the skillet.
7. Garnish with chopped fresh chives and serve immediately.

Nutritional Values (per serving, based on 4 servings):

- Calories: 350
- Fat: 24g
- Carbohydrates: 12g
- Fiber: 4g
- Protein: 24g

Chicken Parmesan (Breaded with Almond Flour)

Ingredients:

- 4 boneless, skinless chicken breasts
- Salt and pepper to taste
- 1 cup almond flour
- 1/2 cup grated Parmesan cheese
- 1 teaspoon dried oregano
- 1 teaspoon dried basil

85

- 1/2 teaspoon garlic powder
- 2 large eggs
- 2 tablespoons olive oil
- 1 1/2 cups marinara sauce (sugar-free preferred)
- 1 cup shredded mozzarella cheese
- Fresh basil, chopped, for garnish

Directions:

1. Preheat your oven to 375°F (190°C). Line a baking sheet with parchment paper or lightly grease a baking dish.
2. Place the chicken breasts between two sheets of plastic wrap and pound them to an even thickness using a meat mallet.
3. Season the chicken breasts with salt and pepper on both sides.
4. In a shallow dish, combine the almond flour, grated Parmesan cheese, dried oregano, dried basil, and garlic powder. Mix well.
5. In another shallow dish, beat the eggs.
6. Dip each chicken breast into the beaten eggs, allowing any excess to drip off, then dredge in the almond flour mixture, pressing gently to coat both sides evenly.
7. Heat the olive oil in a large skillet over medium-high heat. Add the breaded chicken breasts and cook for about 3-4 minutes on each side, or until golden brown. You may need to do this in batches to avoid overcrowding the pan.
8. Transfer the browned chicken breasts to the prepared baking sheet or baking dish.
9. Spoon the marinara sauce evenly over each chicken breast, then sprinkle with shredded mozzarella cheese.
10. Bake in the preheated oven for 20-25 minutes, or until the chicken is cooked through and the cheese is melted and bubbly.
11. Remove from the oven and let cool for a few minutes before serving.
12. Garnish with chopped fresh basil and serve.

Nutritional Values (per serving, based on 4 servings):

- Calories: 450
- Fat: 28g
- Carbohydrates: 10g
- Fiber: 3g
- Protein: 40g

Beef and Broccoli

Ingredients:

- 1 pound flank steak or sirloin, thinly sliced against the grain
- 3 tablespoons soy sauce (or tamari for gluten-free)
- 2 tablespoons oyster sauce
- 2 tablespoons hoisin sauce
- 1 tablespoon cornstarch
- 3 tablespoons water
- 1/4 cup beef broth
- 2 tablespoons olive oil
- 4 cups broccoli florets
- 1 medium onion, sliced
- 3 cloves garlic, minced
- 1 teaspoon fresh ginger, grated
- 1/4 teaspoon red pepper flakes (optional)
- Sesame seeds and sliced green onions for garnish (optional)

Directions:

1. In a medium bowl, combine the sliced beef, 1 tablespoon of soy sauce, and 1 tablespoon of cornstarch. Toss to coat the

beef evenly and set aside for 10-15 minutes to marinate.

2. In a small bowl, mix together the remaining soy sauce, oyster sauce, hoisin sauce, and 3 tablespoons of water. Set aside.

3. Heat 1 tablespoon of olive oil in a large skillet or wok over medium-high heat. Add the broccoli florets and cook for about 3-4 minutes, stirring frequently, until they are bright green and tender-crisp. Remove the broccoli from the skillet and set aside.

4. In the same skillet, add the remaining 1 tablespoon of olive oil. Add the marinated beef in a single layer and cook for about 2-3 minutes on each side, or until browned and cooked through. Remove the beef from the skillet and set aside.

5. Add the sliced onion to the skillet and cook for about 2-3 minutes until softened. Add the minced garlic, grated ginger, and red pepper flakes (if using), and cook for another minute until fragrant.

6. Return the beef and broccoli to the skillet. Pour the sauce mixture over the beef and broccoli, stirring well to coat everything evenly.

7. Add the beef broth to the skillet and bring to a simmer. Cook for another 2-3 minutes, or until the sauce has thickened and the beef and broccoli are heated through.

8. Remove from heat and garnish with sesame seeds and sliced green onions if desired.

9. Serve hot over steamed rice or cauliflower rice for a low-carb option.

Nutritional Values (per serving, based on 4 servings):

- Calories: 350
- Fat: 18g
- Carbohydrates: 16g
- Fiber: 4g
- Protein: 28g

Vegetarian Stuffed Zucchini Boats

Ingredients:

- 4 medium zucchinis
- 1 tablespoon olive oil
- 1 small onion, finely chopped
- 2 cloves garlic, minced
- 1 red bell pepper, diced
- 1 cup cherry tomatoes, halved
- 1 cup cooked quinoa
- 1 can (15 oz) black beans, drained and rinsed
- 1 teaspoon ground cumin
- 1 teaspoon chili powder
- 1/2 teaspoon paprika
- Salt and pepper to taste
- 1/2 cup shredded cheddar cheese (or vegan cheese for a dairy-free option)
- Fresh cilantro, chopped, for garnish
- Lime wedges, for serving

Directions:

1. Preheat your oven to 375°F (190°C). Line a baking sheet with parchment paper or lightly grease a baking dish.

2. Cut the zucchinis in half lengthwise and scoop out the flesh, leaving about 1/4-inch border around the edges to create a boat shape. Set the scooped-out flesh aside.

3. Place the zucchini boats on the prepared baking sheet and brush the insides with a little olive oil. Season with salt and pepper and bake for about 10-15 minutes, or until they start to soften.
4. While the zucchinis are baking, heat the remaining olive oil in a large skillet over medium heat. Add the finely chopped onion and cook until softened, about 5 minutes.
5. Add the minced garlic and cook for another minute until fragrant.
6. Stir in the diced red bell pepper, cherry tomatoes, and the scooped-out zucchini flesh (chopped). Cook for another 5 minutes until the vegetables are tender.
7. Add the cooked quinoa and black beans to the skillet. Stir in the ground cumin, chili powder, paprika, salt, and pepper. Cook for another 3-4 minutes, allowing the flavors to meld.
8. Remove the zucchini boats from the oven and fill each one with the quinoa and vegetable mixture.
9. Sprinkle the shredded cheddar cheese evenly over the top of each stuffed zucchini.
10. Return the zucchini boats to the oven and bake for another 10-15 minutes, or until the cheese is melted and bubbly.
11. Remove from the oven and let cool for a few minutes before serving.
12. Garnish with chopped fresh cilantro and serve with lime wedges on the side.

Nutritional Values (per serving, based on 4 servings):

- Calories: 280
- Fat: 10g
- Carbohydrates: 36g
- Fiber: 10g

- Protein: 12g

Cod with Tomato and Basil

Ingredients:

- 4 cod fillets (about 6 ounces each)
- Salt and pepper to taste
- 2 tablespoons olive oil
- 1 small onion, finely chopped
- 3 cloves garlic, minced
- 1 pint cherry tomatoes, halved
- 1/4 cup dry white wine (optional)
- 1/2 cup vegetable broth
- 1 teaspoon dried oregano
- 1/2 teaspoon red pepper flakes (optional)
- 1/4 cup fresh basil, chopped
- Lemon wedges, for serving

Directions:

1. Pat the cod fillets dry with paper towels and season both sides with salt and pepper.
2. Heat the olive oil in a large skillet over medium-high heat. Add the cod fillets to the skillet and cook for about 3-4 minutes on each side, or until the fish is golden brown and cooked through. Remove the cod from the skillet and set aside.
3. In the same skillet, add the finely chopped onion and cook until softened, about 5 minutes.
4. Add the minced garlic to the skillet and cook for another minute until fragrant.
5. Stir in the halved cherry tomatoes and cook for about 3-4 minutes until they begin to soften.
6. Pour in the dry white wine (if using) and vegetable broth, and stir in the dried

oregano and red pepper flakes (if using). Bring the mixture to a simmer and cook for about 5 minutes, allowing the flavors to meld and the sauce to thicken slightly.

7. Return the cod fillets to the skillet, spooning some of the tomato and basil sauce over the top. Cook for another 2-3 minutes until the fish is heated through.

8. Remove from heat and stir in the chopped fresh basil.

9. Serve the cod fillets with the tomato and basil sauce, garnished with lemon wedges for squeezing over the top.

Nutritional Values (per serving, based on 4 servings):

- Calories: 250
- Fat: 12g
- Carbohydrates: 8g
- Fiber: 2g
- Protein: 28g

Ratatouille

Ingredients:

- 1 eggplant, diced
- 1 zucchini, diced
- 1 yellow squash, diced
- 1 red bell pepper, diced
- 1 yellow bell pepper, diced
- 1 large onion, chopped
- 4 cloves garlic, minced
- 4 tablespoons olive oil, divided
- 1 can (28 oz) crushed tomatoes
- 1 teaspoon dried thyme
- 1 teaspoon dried oregano
- 1/4 teaspoon red pepper flakes (optional)
- Salt and pepper to taste
- 1/4 cup fresh basil, chopped
- 1/4 cup fresh parsley, chopped

Directions:

1. Preheat your oven to 375°F (190°C).

2. In a large bowl, toss the diced eggplant, zucchini, yellow squash, red bell pepper, and yellow bell pepper with 2 tablespoons of olive oil, salt, and pepper. Spread the vegetables in a single layer on a baking sheet and roast in the preheated oven for about 20-25 minutes, or until tender and lightly browned. Stir halfway through roasting.

3. While the vegetables are roasting, heat the remaining 2 tablespoons of olive oil in a large pot over medium heat. Add the chopped onion and cook until softened, about 5 minutes.

4. Add the minced garlic to the pot and cook for another minute until fragrant.

5. Stir in the crushed tomatoes, dried thyme, dried oregano, red pepper flakes (if using), salt, and pepper. Bring the mixture to a simmer and let it cook for about 10 minutes, allowing the flavors to meld.

6. Once the roasted vegetables are done, add them to the pot with the tomato sauce. Stir well to combine.

7. Reduce the heat to low and let the ratatouille simmer for another 10-15 minutes, stirring occasionally.

8. Remove from heat and stir in the chopped fresh basil and parsley.

9. Serve the ratatouille hot, either on its own or over a bed of rice, quinoa, or pasta. Garnish with additional fresh herbs if desired.

Nutritional Values (per serving, based on 4 servings):

- Calories: 200
- Fat: 14g

- Carbohydrates: 18g
- Fiber: 6g
- Protein: 4g

Slow Cooker Pulled Pork

Ingredients:

- 4 pounds pork shoulder (pork butt), trimmed of excess fat
- 1 large onion, sliced
- 4 cloves garlic, minced
- 1 cup barbecue sauce (sugar-free if preferred)
- 1/2 cup apple cider vinegar
- 1/4 cup chicken broth
- 2 tablespoons brown sugar (or a sugar substitute)
- 1 tablespoon paprika
- 1 tablespoon chili powder
- 1 teaspoon ground cumin
- 1 teaspoon dried oregano
- 1 teaspoon salt
- 1/2 teaspoon black pepper
- 1/4 teaspoon cayenne pepper (optional)
- 1 tablespoon olive oil

Directions:

1. In a small bowl, combine the paprika, chili powder, ground cumin, dried oregano, salt, black pepper, and cayenne pepper (if using). Rub this spice mixture all over the pork shoulder.
2. Heat the olive oil in a large skillet over medium-high heat. Sear the pork shoulder on all sides until browned, about 3-4 minutes per side. Remove from the skillet and set aside.
3. Place the sliced onion and minced garlic in the bottom of the slow cooker. Lay the seared pork shoulder on top of the onions.

4. In a bowl, whisk together the barbecue sauce, apple cider vinegar, chicken broth, and brown sugar (or sugar substitute). Pour this mixture over the pork shoulder in the slow cooker.
5. Cover and cook on low for 8-10 hours, or until the pork is very tender and easily shreds with a fork.
6. Once cooked, remove the pork from the slow cooker and place it on a large cutting board. Use two forks to shred the pork, discarding any large pieces of fat.
7. Return the shredded pork to the slow cooker and stir it into the sauce. Let it cook on low for another 30 minutes to absorb the flavors.
8. Serve the pulled pork on buns, in tacos, or over rice. Top with additional barbecue sauce if desired.

Nutritional Values (per serving, based on 8 servings):

- Calories: 350
- Fat: 18g
- Carbohydrates: 13g
- Fiber: 2g
- Protein: 30g

Low-Carb Jambalaya

Ingredients:

- 1 pound chicken breast, diced
- 1/2 pound andouille sausage, sliced
- 1/2 pound shrimp, peeled and deveined
- 2 tablespoons olive oil
- 1 large onion, chopped
- 1 green bell pepper, chopped
- 1 red bell pepper, chopped
- 3 cloves garlic, minced
- 1 can (14.5 oz) diced tomatoes

- 1/2 cup chicken broth
- 2 tablespoons tomato paste
- 1 teaspoon dried thyme
- 1 teaspoon dried oregano
- 1 teaspoon smoked paprika
- 1/2 teaspoon cayenne pepper (optional, for heat)
- 1 teaspoon salt
- 1/2 teaspoon black pepper
- 4 cups cauliflower rice
- 2 green onions, chopped, for garnish
- Fresh parsley, chopped, for garnish

Directions:

1. In a large skillet or Dutch oven, heat 1 tablespoon of olive oil over medium-high heat. Add the diced chicken breast and cook until browned and cooked through, about 5-7 minutes. Remove the chicken from the skillet and set aside.
2. In the same skillet, add the sliced andouille sausage and cook until browned, about 4-5 minutes. Remove the sausage from the skillet and set aside with the chicken.
3. Add the remaining tablespoon of olive oil to the skillet. Add the chopped onion, green bell pepper, and red bell pepper. Cook until the vegetables are softened, about 5 minutes.
4. Add the minced garlic and cook for another minute until fragrant.
5. Stir in the diced tomatoes, chicken broth, tomato paste, dried thyme, dried oregano, smoked paprika, cayenne pepper (if using), salt, and black pepper. Bring the mixture to a simmer.
6. Return the cooked chicken and sausage to the skillet. Stir to combine and let the mixture simmer for about 10 minutes, allowing the flavors to meld.
7. Add the shrimp to the skillet and cook for about 5 minutes, or until the shrimp are pink and opaque.
8. Stir in the cauliflower rice and cook for another 5 minutes, or until the cauliflower rice is tender and heated through.
9. Remove from heat and garnish with chopped green onions and fresh parsley.
10. Serve the low-carb jambalaya hot and enjoy.

Nutritional Values (per serving, based on 6 servings):

- Calories: 320
- Fat: 15g
- Carbohydrates: 12g
- Fiber: 4g
- Protein: 34g

Roast Turkey with Low-Carb Stuffing

Ingredients:

For the Turkey:

- 1 whole turkey (10-12 pounds)
- 1/4 cup olive oil or melted butter
- Salt and pepper to taste
- 1 tablespoon dried thyme
- 1 tablespoon dried rosemary
- 1 tablespoon dried sage
- 1 lemon, halved
- 1 onion, quartered
- 4 cloves garlic
- 2 cups chicken broth

For the Low-Carb Stuffing:

- 1 head cauliflower, chopped into small florets
- 1/2 cup almond flour
- 1/4 cup grated Parmesan cheese

- 1/4 cup butter, melted
- 1 small onion, finely chopped
- 2 cloves garlic, minced
- 1 cup celery, chopped
- 1/2 cup mushrooms, chopped
- 1/4 cup fresh parsley, chopped
- 1 teaspoon dried thyme
- 1 teaspoon dried rosemary
- 1 teaspoon dried sage
- Salt and pepper to taste

Directions:

Preparing the Turkey:

1. Preheat your oven to 325°F (165°C).
2. Rinse the turkey inside and out, then pat it dry with paper towels. Place the turkey on a rack in a large roasting pan.
3. Rub the olive oil or melted butter all over the turkey, including under the skin. Season generously with salt, pepper, dried thyme, dried rosemary, and dried sage.
4. Stuff the cavity of the turkey with the lemon halves, quartered onion, and garlic cloves.
5. Tie the legs together with kitchen twine and tuck the wing tips under the body of the turkey.
6. Pour 2 cups of chicken broth into the bottom of the roasting pan.

Preparing the Low-Carb Stuffing:

1. In a large skillet, melt the butter over medium heat. Add the finely chopped onion, minced garlic, chopped celery, and chopped mushrooms. Cook until the vegetables are softened, about 5-7 minutes.
2. In a large bowl, combine the cooked vegetables with the chopped cauliflower florets, almond flour, grated Parmesan cheese, fresh parsley, dried thyme, dried rosemary, dried sage, salt, and pepper. Mix well to combine.
3. Spread the stuffing mixture in an even layer in a baking dish.

Roasting the Turkey:

1. Place the turkey in the preheated oven and roast for about 3 to 3 1/2 hours, or until the internal temperature reaches 165°F (75°C) in the thickest part of the thigh. Baste the turkey with the pan juices every 30 minutes.
2. During the last hour of roasting, place the stuffing in the oven and bake for about 45-50 minutes, or until the top is golden brown and the cauliflower is tender.

Serving:

1. Remove the turkey from the oven and let it rest for about 20-30 minutes before carving.
2. Serve the roast turkey with the low-carb stuffing on the side.

Nutritional Values (per serving, based on 12 servings):

Turkey:

- Calories: 350
- Fat: 18g
- Carbohydrates: 1g
- Fiber: 0g
- Protein: 43g

Stuffing:

- Calories: 150
- Fat: 10g

- Carbohydrates: 8g
- Fiber: 3g
- Protein: 6g

Herb-Crusted Pork Chops with Cauliflower Mash

Ingredients:

- 4 bone-in pork chops (about 1-inch thick)
- 2 tablespoons olive oil
- 1/4 cup grated Parmesan cheese
- 2 tablespoons almond flour
- 1 tablespoon fresh rosemary, chopped
- 1 tablespoon fresh thyme, chopped
- 1 tablespoon fresh parsley, chopped
- 2 cloves garlic, minced
- Salt and pepper to taste

Directions:

1. Preheat your oven to 375°F (190°C). Line a baking sheet with parchment paper or lightly grease a baking dish.
2. In a small bowl, combine the grated Parmesan cheese, almond flour, chopped rosemary, chopped thyme, chopped parsley, minced garlic, salt, and pepper.
3. Rub the olive oil all over the pork chops. Then press the herb mixture onto both sides of each pork chop, ensuring they are well-coated.
4. Place the pork chops on the prepared baking sheet and bake in the preheated oven for about 20-25 minutes, or until the internal temperature reaches 145°F (63°C) and the crust is golden brown.
5. Remove from the oven and let the pork chops rest for a few minutes before serving.

Nutritional Values (per serving):

- Calories: 350
- Fat: 22g
- Carbohydrates: 3g
- Fiber: 1g
- Protein: 32g

Cauliflower Mash Recipe

Ingredients:

- 1 large head cauliflower, cut into florets
- 1/4 cup heavy cream
- 2 tablespoons butter
- 1/4 cup grated Parmesan cheese
- Salt and pepper to taste
- Fresh chives, chopped, for garnish

Directions:

1. While the pork chops are baking, steam or boil the cauliflower florets until tender, about 10-15 minutes. Drain well.
2. Transfer the cauliflower to a food processor. Add the heavy cream, butter, grated Parmesan cheese, salt, and pepper.
3. Process until smooth and creamy. Taste and adjust seasoning if needed.
4. Transfer the cauliflower mash to a serving bowl and garnish with chopped fresh chives.

Nutritional Values (per serving):

- Calories: 120
- Fat: 8g
- Carbohydrates: 10g
- Fiber: 4g
- Protein: 4g

Lemon Basil Chicken over Spinach

Ingredients:

- 4 boneless, skinless chicken breasts
- Salt and pepper to taste
- 2 tablespoons olive oil
- 3 cloves garlic, minced
- 1/2 cup chicken broth
- 1/4 cup fresh lemon juice (about 2 lemons)
- 1/4 cup fresh basil, chopped
- 1 teaspoon lemon zest
- 6 cups fresh spinach leaves
- Lemon slices, for garnish

Directions:

1. Season the chicken breasts with salt and pepper on both sides.
2. Heat the olive oil in a large skillet over medium-high heat. Add the chicken breasts and cook for about 6-7 minutes on each side, or until golden brown and cooked through. Remove the chicken from the skillet and set aside.
3. In the same skillet, add the minced garlic and cook for about 1 minute until fragrant.
4. Pour in the chicken broth and lemon juice, scraping up any browned bits from the bottom of the skillet. Bring to a simmer and cook for about 2-3 minutes, allowing the sauce to reduce slightly.
5. Stir in the chopped basil and lemon zest.
6. Return the chicken breasts to the skillet, spooning the sauce over the top. Cook for another 2-3 minutes until the chicken is heated through and well-coated with the sauce.
7. While the chicken is finishing, place the fresh spinach leaves on serving plates.
8. Serve the lemon basil chicken over the bed of fresh spinach, garnished with lemon slices.

Nutritional Values (per serving):

- Calories: 280
- Fat: 12g
- Carbohydrates: 4g
- Fiber: 2g
- Protein: 36g

Beef Stir-Fry with Bell Peppers and Snow Peas

Ingredients:

- 1 pound flank steak or sirloin, thinly sliced against the grain
- 2 tablespoons soy sauce (or tamari for gluten-free)
- 1 tablespoon cornstarch
- 2 tablespoons vegetable oil
- 1 red bell pepper, thinly sliced
- 1 yellow bell pepper, thinly sliced
- 1 cup snow peas, trimmed
- 1 small onion, thinly sliced
- 3 cloves garlic, minced
- 1 tablespoon fresh ginger, grated
- 1/4 cup low-sodium beef broth
- 2 tablespoons hoisin sauce
- 1 tablespoon oyster sauce
- 1 tablespoon rice vinegar
- 1 teaspoon sesame oil
- Sesame seeds and sliced green onions for garnish (optional)

Directions:

1. In a medium bowl, combine the sliced beef, soy sauce, and cornstarch. Toss to

94

coat the beef evenly and set aside for 10-15 minutes to marinate.

2. Heat 1 tablespoon of vegetable oil in a large skillet or wok over medium-high heat. Add the marinated beef and stir-fry for about 2-3 minutes, or until browned and cooked through. Remove the beef from the skillet and set aside.

3. In the same skillet, add the remaining 1 tablespoon of vegetable oil. Add the sliced red bell pepper, yellow bell pepper, snow peas, and onion. Stir-fry for about 3-4 minutes, or until the vegetables are tender-crisp.

4. Add the minced garlic and grated ginger to the skillet and cook for another minute until fragrant.

5. In a small bowl, whisk together the beef broth, hoisin sauce, oyster sauce, and rice vinegar. Pour the sauce into the skillet and stir to combine with the vegetables.

6. Return the cooked beef to the skillet and toss to coat with the sauce. Cook for another 2-3 minutes, or until the beef is heated through and the sauce has thickened.

7. Remove from heat and drizzle with sesame oil.

8. Serve the beef stir-fry hot, garnished with sesame seeds and sliced green onions if desired.

Nutritional Values (per serving, based on 4 servings):

- Calories: 300
- Fat: 16g
- Carbohydrates: 12g
- Fiber: 3g
- Protein: 28g

Grilled Salmon with Asparagus and Lemon-Dill Sauce

Ingredients:

- 4 salmon fillets (about 6 ounces each)
- Salt and pepper to taste
- 2 tablespoons olive oil
- 1 pound asparagus, trimmed
- 1 lemon, thinly sliced

For the Lemon-Dill Sauce:

- 1/2 cup Greek yogurt (plain, unsweetened)
- 2 tablespoons fresh dill, chopped
- 2 tablespoons fresh lemon juice
- 1 teaspoon lemon zest
- 1 clove garlic, minced
- Salt and pepper to taste

Directions:

1. Preheat your grill to medium-high heat.

2. Season the salmon fillets with salt and pepper on both sides. Drizzle with 1 tablespoon of olive oil.

3. Toss the asparagus with the remaining 1 tablespoon of olive oil and season with salt and pepper.

4. Place the salmon fillets and asparagus on the grill. Grill the salmon for about 4-5 minutes per side, or until the fish is opaque and flakes easily with a fork. Grill the asparagus for about 3-4 minutes per side, or until tender and slightly charred.

5. While the salmon and asparagus are grilling, prepare the lemon-dill sauce. In a small bowl, combine the Greek yogurt,

chopped dill, lemon juice, lemon zest, minced garlic, salt, and pepper. Mix well until all ingredients are evenly incorporated.

6. Once the salmon and asparagus are done, remove them from the grill and let them rest for a few minutes.

7. Serve the grilled salmon with the asparagus, drizzled with the lemon-dill sauce. Garnish with lemon slices if desired.

Nutritional Values (per serving, based on 4 servings):

- Calories: 350
- Fat: 22g
- Carbohydrates: 7g
- Fiber: 3g
- Protein: 30g

Vegetable and Chickpea Curry with Cauliflower Rice

Ingredients:

For the Curry:

- 2 tablespoons olive oil
- 1 large onion, chopped
- 3 cloves garlic, minced
- 1 tablespoon fresh ginger, grated
- 1 red bell pepper, diced
- 1 yellow bell pepper, diced
- 1 zucchini, diced
- 1 cup carrots, sliced
- 1 can (15 oz) chickpeas, drained and rinsed
- 1 can (14.5 oz) diced tomatoes
- 1 can (14 oz) coconut milk
- 2 tablespoons curry powder
- 1 teaspoon ground cumin
- 1 teaspoon ground coriander
- 1/2 teaspoon turmeric
- 1/2 teaspoon cayenne pepper (optional, for heat)
- Salt and pepper to taste
- 1 cup fresh spinach leaves
- Fresh cilantro, chopped, for garnish

For the Cauliflower Rice:

- 1 large head cauliflower, cut into florets
- 1 tablespoon olive oil
- Salt and pepper to taste

Directions:

Preparing the Curry:

1. Heat the olive oil in a large skillet or Dutch oven over medium heat. Add the chopped onion and cook until softened, about 5 minutes.

2. Add the minced garlic and grated ginger to the skillet and cook for another minute until fragrant.

3. Stir in the diced red bell pepper, yellow bell pepper, zucchini, and carrots. Cook for about 5-7 minutes, or until the vegetables begin to soften.

4. Add the chickpeas, diced tomatoes, coconut milk, curry powder, ground cumin, ground coriander, turmeric, cayenne pepper (if using), salt, and pepper. Stir well to combine.

5. Bring the mixture to a simmer and let it cook for about 15-20 minutes, stirring occasionally, until the vegetables are tender and the flavors have melded together.

6. Stir in the fresh spinach leaves and cook for another 2-3 minutes until wilted.

Preparing the Cauliflower Rice:

1. While the curry is simmering, prepare the cauliflower rice. Pulse the cauliflower florets in a food processor until they resemble rice grains.
2. Heat the olive oil in a large skillet over medium heat. Add the cauliflower rice and season with salt and pepper. Cook for about 5-7 minutes, stirring frequently, until the cauliflower is tender.

Serving:

- Serve the vegetable and chickpea curry over a bed of cauliflower rice.
- Garnish with chopped fresh cilantro and enjoy.

Nutritional Values (per serving, based on 4 servings):

- Calories: 320
- Fat: 18g
- Carbohydrates: 30g
- Fiber: 10g
- Protein: 10g

Almond and Chia Seed Pudding

Ingredients:

- 2 cups unsweetened almond milk
- 1/2 cup chia seeds
- 1/4 cup almond butter
- 2 tablespoons maple syrup or honey (optional, for sweetness)
- 1 teaspoon vanilla extract
- Fresh berries, for topping
- Sliced almonds, for topping

Directions:

1. In a large mixing bowl, combine the unsweetened almond milk, chia seeds, almond butter, maple syrup or honey (if using), and vanilla extract. Stir well to ensure all ingredients are thoroughly mixed.
2. Cover the bowl and refrigerate for at least 4 hours, or overnight, to allow the chia seeds to absorb the liquid and the pudding to thicken. Stir occasionally during the first hour to prevent clumping.
3. Once the pudding has thickened, give it a good stir to ensure a smooth consistency.
4. Spoon the chia seed pudding into serving bowls or jars.
5. Top with fresh berries and sliced almonds before serving.

Nutritional Values (per serving, based on 4 servings):

- Calorics: 210
- Fat: 14g
- Carbohydrates: 16g
- Fiber: 10g
- Protein: 6g

Veggie Chips and Guacamole

Ingredients:

- 1 large zucchini, thinly sliced
- 1 large sweet potato, thinly sliced
- 1 large beet, thinly sliced
- 2 tablespoons olive oil
- Salt and pepper to taste
- 1 teaspoon paprika (optional)

- 1 teaspoon garlic powder (optional)
- 3 ripe avocados
- 1 small red onion, finely chopped
- 1 medium tomato, diced
- 1 jalapeño, seeded and finely chopped
- 2 cloves garlic, minced
- 1/4 cup fresh cilantro, chopped
- Juice of 2 limes
- Salt and pepper to taste

Directions:

For the Veggie Chips:

1. Preheat your oven to 375°F (190°C).
2. Line two baking sheets with parchment paper.
3. In a large bowl, toss the thinly sliced zucchini, sweet potato, and beet with olive oil.
4. Season with salt, pepper, paprika, and garlic powder if using.
5. Arrange the vegetable slices in a single layer on the prepared baking sheets, ensuring they do not overlap.
6. Bake in the preheated oven for about 20-30 minutes, or until the chips are crisp and lightly browned. Flip the slices halfway through baking to ensure even cooking. Keep an eye on them as cooking times may vary depending on the thickness of the slices.
7. Once done, remove the veggie chips from the oven and let them cool on a wire rack.

For the Guacamole:

1. Cut the avocados in half, remove the pits, and scoop the flesh into a medium bowl.
2. Mash the avocados with a fork or potato masher until smooth but still slightly chunky.

3. Add the finely chopped red onion, diced tomato, chopped jalapeño, minced garlic, and fresh cilantro to the bowl. Stir to combine.
4. Squeeze the juice of the limes over the guacamole and season with salt and pepper to taste. Mix well.
5. Serve the veggie chips alongside the guacamole as a healthy and delicious snack or appetizer.

Nutritional Values (per serving, based on 4 servings):

- Calories: 220
- Fat: 16g
- Carbohydrates: 18g
- Fiber: 7g
- Protein: 3g

Mixed Nuts and Seeds

Ingredients:

- 1 cup almonds
- 1 cup cashews
- 1/2 cup walnuts
- 1/2 cup pecans
- 1/4 cup pumpkin seeds
- 1/4 cup sunflower seeds
- 2 tablespoons flaxseeds
- 1 tablespoon chia seeds
- 2 tablespoons olive oil
- 1 teaspoon sea salt
- 1 teaspoon smoked paprika (optional)
- 1/2 teaspoon garlic powder (optional)

Directions:

1. Preheat your oven to 350°F (175°C).
2. Line a baking sheet with parchment paper.

3. In a large bowl, combine the almonds, cashews, walnuts, pecans, pumpkin seeds, sunflower seeds, flaxseeds, and chia seeds.
4. Drizzle the olive oil over the nut and seed mixture and toss to coat evenly.
5. Season with sea salt, smoked paprika, and garlic powder if using. Toss again to distribute the seasoning evenly.
6. Spread the mixture in a single layer on the prepared baking sheet.
7. Bake in the preheated oven for 15-20 minutes, stirring halfway through, until the nuts are lightly toasted and fragrant.
8. Remove from the oven and let cool completely.
9. Store in an airtight container for up to two weeks.

Nutritional Values (per serving, based on 8 servings):

- Calories: 200
- Fat: 18g
- Carbohydrates: 6g
- Fiber: 4g
- Protein: 6g

Cheese and Fruit Platter

Ingredients:

- 8 ounces sharp cheddar cheese, sliced
- 8 ounces brie cheese, sliced
- 8 ounces gouda cheese, sliced
- 1 cup grapes (red or green)
- 1 apple, sliced
- 1 pear, sliced
- 1/2 cup dried apricots
- 1/2 cup dried cranberries

- 1/2 cup mixed nuts (optional)
- Crackers or baguette slices for serving
- Fresh herbs for garnish (optional)

Directions:

1. Arrange the sliced cheddar, brie, and gouda cheeses on a large serving platter.
2. Place the grapes, apple slices, and pear slices around the cheese.
3. Add the dried apricots and dried cranberries to the platter.
4. If using, sprinkle the mixed nuts around the platter for added texture and flavor.
5. Arrange crackers or baguette slices around the edges of the platter or in a separate bowl.
6. Garnish with fresh herbs for an added touch of elegance (optional).
7. Serve immediately or cover and refrigerate until ready to serve.

Nutritional Values (per serving, based on 8 servings):

- Calories: 250
- Fat: 18g
- Carbohydrates: 14g
- Fiber: 2g
- Protein: 10g

Peanut Butter Celery Sticks

Ingredients:

- 6 large celery stalks
- 1/2 cup natural peanut butter
- 1/4 cup raisins or dried cranberries (optional)
- 1/4 cup chopped nuts (optional)

Directions:

1. Wash the celery stalks thoroughly and cut them into 3-inch pieces.
2. Spread about 1 tablespoon of peanut butter into the groove of each celery piece.
3. Top with raisins or dried cranberries, if using, for added sweetness.
4. Sprinkle with chopped nuts, if using, for extra crunch and flavor.
5. Arrange the peanut butter celery sticks on a serving plate and serve immediately.

Nutritional Values (per serving, based on 6 servings):

- Calories: 150
- Fat: 12g
- Carbohydrates: 8g
- Fiber: 3g
- Protein: 5g

Kale Chips

Ingredients:

- 1 large bunch of kale
- 2 tablespoons olive oil
- 1 teaspoon sea salt
- 1/2 teaspoon garlic powder (optional)
- 1/2 teaspoon smoked paprika (optional)

Directions:

1. Preheat your oven to 300°F (150°C). Line a baking sheet with parchment paper.
2. Wash and thoroughly dry the kale. Remove the tough stems and tear the leaves into bite-sized pieces.
3. Place the kale pieces in a large bowl. Drizzle with olive oil and sprinkle with sea salt, garlic powder, and smoked paprika if using.

4. Toss the kale thoroughly to ensure all the pieces are evenly coated with oil and seasoning.
5. Spread the kale in a single layer on the prepared baking sheet.
6. Bake in the preheated oven for 20-25 minutes, or until the kale is crispy. Be sure to check frequently to prevent burning.
7. Remove from the oven and let cool completely. The kale chips will continue to crisp up as they cool.
8. Serve immediately or store in an airtight container for up to a week.

Nutritional Values (per serving, based on 4 servings):

- Calories: 80
- Fat: 5g
- Carbohydrates: 7g
- Fiber: 2g
- Protein: 3g

Spiced Pumpkin Seeds

Ingredients:

- 1 cup raw pumpkin seeds
- 1 tablespoon olive oil
- 1/2 teaspoon sea salt
- 1/2 teaspoon paprika
- 1/4 teaspoon cayenne pepper (optional, for heat)
- 1/4 teaspoon garlic powder
- 1/4 teaspoon ground cumin

Directions:

1. Preheat your oven to 300°F (150°C). Line a baking sheet with parchment paper.

2. In a medium bowl, combine the pumpkin seeds, olive oil, sea salt, paprika, cayenne pepper (if using), garlic powder, and ground cumin. Toss well to coat the seeds evenly with the oil and spices.
3. Spread the seasoned pumpkin seeds in a single layer on the prepared baking sheet.
4. Bake in the preheated oven for about 20-25 minutes, or until the seeds are golden brown and crispy. Stir the seeds halfway through the baking time to ensure even toasting.
5. Remove the pumpkin seeds from the oven and let them cool completely on the baking sheet.
6. Once cooled, transfer the spiced pumpkin seeds to an airtight container for storage.

Nutritional Values (per serving, based on 4 servings):

- Calories: 140
- Fat: 11g
- Carbohydrates: 4g
- Fiber: 2g
- Protein: 6g

Hard-Boiled Eggs

Ingredients:

- 6 large eggs
- Water, for boiling
- Ice, for an ice bath

Directions:

1. Place the eggs in a single layer at the bottom of a large pot. Add enough cold water to cover the eggs by about an inch.
2. Over high heat, bring the water to a rolling boil. Once the water reaches a boil, cover the pot with a lid and remove it from the heat.
3. Let the eggs sit in the hot water for 10-12 minutes, depending on your desired level of doneness (10 minutes for slightly softer yolks, 12 minutes for fully firm yolks).
4. While the eggs are cooking, prepare an ice bath by filling a large bowl with ice and water.
5. After the eggs have finished cooking, use a slotted spoon to transfer them to the ice bath. Let the eggs sit in the ice bath for at least 5 minutes to cool completely.
6. Once cooled, gently tap the eggs on a hard surface to crack the shells. Peel the eggs and serve immediately or store in the refrigerator for up to a week.

Nutritional Values (per serving, based on 1 egg):

- Calories: 70
- Fat: 5g
- Carbohydrates: 1g
- Fiber: 0g
- Protein: 6g

Caprese Salad Skewers

Ingredients:

- 1 pint cherry tomatoes
- 1 pound fresh mozzarella balls (bocconcini)
- Fresh basil leaves
- 2 tablespoons balsamic glaze

- 2 tablespoons extra virgin olive oil
- Salt and pepper to taste
- Wooden skewers

Directions:

1. Rinse the cherry tomatoes and fresh basil leaves. Drain the mozzarella balls and pat them dry with a paper towel.
2. To assemble the skewers, start by threading a cherry tomato onto a wooden skewer, followed by a fresh basil leaf and a mozzarella ball. Repeat until the skewer is full, leaving a small space at the end for handling. Repeat with the remaining ingredients and skewers.
3. Arrange the assembled skewers on a serving platter.
4. Drizzle the balsamic glaze and extra virgin olive oil over the skewers.
5. Season with salt and pepper to taste.
6. Serve immediately or refrigerate until ready to serve.

Nutritional Values (per serving, based on 8 servings):

- Calories: 120
- Fat: 9g
- Carbohydrates: 3g
- Fiber: 1g
- Protein: 6g

Greek Yogurt Dip with Veggies

Ingredients:

- 2 cups plain Greek yogurt
- 1 cucumber, finely chopped
- 1 small red bell pepper, finely chopped
- 1 small carrot, finely grated

- 2 cloves garlic, minced
- 2 tablespoons fresh dill, chopped
- 2 tablespoons fresh parsley, chopped
- 1 tablespoon fresh lemon juice
- 1 teaspoon salt
- 1/2 teaspoon black pepper
- Assorted fresh vegetables for dipping (carrot sticks, celery sticks, bell pepper strips, cucumber slices, cherry tomatoes, etc.)

Directions:

1. In a medium bowl, combine the plain Greek yogurt, finely chopped cucumber, finely chopped red bell pepper, finely grated carrot, and minced garlic.
2. Add the chopped fresh dill, chopped fresh parsley, fresh lemon juice, salt, and black pepper. Stir well to combine all the ingredients.
3. Cover the bowl and refrigerate the dip for at least 30 minutes to allow the flavors to meld together.
4. Arrange the assorted fresh vegetables on a serving platter
5. Serve the Greek yogurt dip with the fresh vegetables for dipping.

Nutritional Values (per serving, based on 8 servings):

Calories: 60

Fat: 1.5g

Carbohydrates: 5g

Fiber: 1g

Protein: 6g

CHAPTER 4
DESSERTS

In this chapter, you'll find an array of delightful dessert recipes that are not only delicious but also mindful of your dietary needs. These treats are designed to satisfy your sweet tooth without compromising on health. From rich and decadent options to light and refreshing bites, each recipe offers a balance of flavors and nutrition. Whether you're looking for a guilt-free indulgence or a special treat to share with loved ones, these desserts are sure to impress. Get ready to explore a world of sweet possibilities that you can enjoy any time of the day.

Flourless Chocolate Cake

Ingredients:

- 1 cup semisweet or dark chocolate chips
- 1/2 cup unsalted butter, cut into pieces
- 3/4 cup granulated sugar
- 1/4 teaspoon salt
- 1 teaspoon vanilla extract
- 3 large eggs
- 1/2 cup unsweetened cocoa powder

Directions:

1. Preheat your oven to 375°F (190°C). Grease an 8-inch round cake pan and line the bottom with parchment paper.
2. In a microwave-safe bowl, combine the chocolate chips and butter. Microwave in 30-second intervals, stirring after each, until the chocolate and butter are completely melted and smooth.
3. Add the granulated sugar, salt, and vanilla extract to the melted chocolate mixture, stirring until well combined.
4. Add the eggs one at a time, beating well after each addition.
5. Sift the unsweetened cocoa powder into the mixture and stir until just combined.
6. Pour the batter into the prepared cake pan and smooth the top with a spatula.
7. Bake in the preheated oven for 20-25 minutes, or until the cake has set and a toothpick inserted into the center comes out with a few moist crumbs.
8. Let the cake cool in the pan for 10 minutes, then run a knife around the edge of the pan to loosen the cake. Invert the cake onto a serving plate and remove the parchment paper.
9. Allow the cake to cool completely before scrving. Dust with powdered sugar or cocoa powder, if desired.

Nutritional Values (per serving, based on 8 servings):

- Calories: 240
- Fat: 16g
- Carbohydrates: 26g
- Fiber: 3g
- Protein: 4g

Baked Apples with Cinnamon

Ingredients:

- 4 large apples (such as Granny Smith or Honeycrisp)

- 1/4 cup chopped nuts (such as walnuts or pecans)
- 1/4 cup raisins or dried cranberries
- 2 tablespoons honey or maple syrup
- 1 teaspoon ground cinnamon
- 1/2 teaspoon ground nutmeg
- 1 tablespoon unsalted butter, cut into small pieces
- 1/2 cup apple juice or water

Directions:

1. Preheat your oven to 350°F (175°C). Grease a baking dish with a little butter or oil.
2. Core the apples, making sure to leave the bottoms intact to hold the filling. Use a spoon or melon baller to scoop out the seeds and create a cavity in the center of each apple.
3. In a small bowl, combine the chopped nuts, raisins or dried cranberries, honey or maple syrup, ground cinnamon, and ground nutmeg. Mix well.
4. Stuff each apple with the nut and raisin mixture, pressing it down into the cavity.
5. Place the stuffed apples in the prepared baking dish. Dot the tops of the apples with the small pieces of butter.
6. Pour the apple juice or water into the baking dish around the apples.
7. Bake in the preheated oven for 40-45 minutes, or until the apples are tender and the filling is bubbly.
8. Remove from the oven and let cool slightly before serving.

Nutritional Values (per serving, based on 4 servings):

- Calories: 180
- Fat: 6g
- Carbohydrates: 33g
- Fiber: 5g
- Protein: 1g

Almond Joy Bars (Sugar-Free)

Ingredients:

- 1 cup unsweetened shredded coconut
- 1/4 cup coconut oil, melted
- 1/4 cup sugar-free maple syrup
- 1 teaspoon vanilla extract
- 1/4 cup whole almonds
- 1 cup sugar-free dark chocolate chips

Directions:

1. Line an 8x8-inch baking dish with parchment paper, leaving an overhang on the sides for easy removal.
2. In a medium bowl, combine the unsweetened shredded coconut, melted coconut oil, sugar-free maple syrup, and vanilla extract. Stir until the mixture is well combined and holds together when pressed.
3. Transfer the coconut mixture to the prepared baking dish. Press it firmly and evenly into the bottom of the dish.
4. Arrange the whole almonds evenly over the top of the coconut mixture, pressing them slightly into the surface.
5. In a microwave-safe bowl, melt the sugar-free dark chocolate chips in 30-second intervals, stirring after each, until completely melted and smooth.
6. Pour the melted chocolate over the almond and coconut layer, spreading it evenly with a spatula to cover the entire surface.

7. Refrigerate the dish for at least 1 hour, or until the chocolate is set and the bars are firm.

8. Once set, lift the bars out of the dish using the parchment paper overhang and place them on a cutting board. Cut into 12 bars.

9. Store the Almond Joy bars in an airtight container in the refrigerator for up to a week.

Nutritional Values (per serving, based on 12 servings):

- Calories: 180
- Fat: 16g
- Carbohydrates: 5g
- Fiber: 3g
- Protein: 2g

Strawberry Cheesecake (Sugar-Free)

Ingredients:

For the Crust:

- 1 1/2 cups almond flour
- 1/4 cup melted butter
- 2 tablespoons sugar-free sweetener (such as erythritol or stevia)
- 1/2 teaspoon vanilla extract

For the Cheesecake Filling:

- 16 ounces cream cheese, softened
- 1/2 cup sugar-free sweetener
- 1 teaspoon vanilla extract
- 2 large eggs
- 1/4 cup sour cream

For the Strawberry Topping:

- 1 cup fresh strawberries, sliced
- 2 tablespoons sugar-free sweetener
- 1 tablespoon lemon juice

Directions:

1. Preheat your oven to 325°F (163°C). Grease a 9-inch springform pan and line the bottom with parchment paper.

2. In a medium bowl, mix together the almond flour, melted butter, sugar-free sweetener, and vanilla extract until the mixture is well combined and crumbly.

3. Press the crust mixture evenly into the bottom of the prepared springform pan. Bake in the preheated oven for 10 minutes, then remove and let cool while you prepare the filling.

4. In a large bowl, beat the softened cream cheese and sugar-free sweetener together until smooth and creamy. Add the vanilla extract and mix until well combined.

5. Add the eggs one at a time, beating well after each addition. Finally, add the sour cream and mix until the filling is smooth and well combined.

6. Pour the cheesecake filling over the cooled crust and spread it evenly with a spatula.

7. Bake in the preheated oven for 40-45 minutes, or until the center is set and the edges are lightly browned. Turn off the oven and let the cheesecake cool in the oven with the door slightly open for about an hour.

8. While the cheesecake is cooling, prepare the strawberry topping. In a small saucepan, combine the sliced strawberries, sugar-free sweetener, and lemon juice. Cook over medium heat, stirring occasionally, until the strawberries release their juices and the mixture thickens slightly, about 5-7 minutes. Remove from heat and let cool.

9. Once the cheesecake has cooled to room temperature, spread the strawberry topping evenly over the top.

10. Refrigerate the cheesecake for at least 4 hours, or overnight, to allow it to set completely.

11. Before serving, run a knife around the edge of the springform pan to loosen the cheesecake. Remove the sides of the pan and transfer the cheesecake to a serving plate.

Nutritional Values (per serving, based on 12 servings):

- Calories: 280
- Fat: 25g
- Carbohydrates: 6g
- Fiber: 2g
- Protein: 7g

Coconut Flour Brownies

Ingredients:

- 1/2 cup unsalted butter, melted
- 1/2 cup sugar-free sweetener (such as erythritol or stevia)
- 4 large eggs
- 1 teaspoon vanilla extract
- 1/2 cup unsweetened cocoa powder
- 1/4 cup coconut flour
- 1/2 teaspoon baking powder
- 1/4 teaspoon salt
- 1/2 cup sugar-free chocolate chips (optional)

Directions:

1. Preheat your oven to 350°F (175°C). Grease an 8x8-inch baking dish or line it with parchment paper.

2. In a large mixing bowl, combine the melted butter and sugar-free sweetener. Mix well until the sweetener is fully dissolved.

3. Add the eggs one at a time, beating well after each addition. Stir in the vanilla extract.

4. Sift the unsweetened cocoa powder, coconut flour, baking powder, and salt into the bowl. Mix until all ingredients are well combined and the batter is smooth.

5. If using, fold in the sugar-free chocolate chips.

6. Pour the batter into the prepared baking dish and spread it out evenly with a spatula.

7. Bake in the preheated oven for 20-25 minutes, or until a toothpick inserted into the center comes out with a few moist crumbs. Be careful not to overbake, as the brownies will continue to set as they cool.

8. Remove from the oven and let the brownies cool completely in the baking dish.

9. Once cooled, cut into squares and serve.

Nutritional Values (per serving, based on 12 servings):

- Calories: 120
- Fat: 9g
- Carbohydrates: 5g
- Fiber: 2g
- Protein: 3g

Berry and Mascarpone Tart

Ingredients:

For the Crust:

- 1 1/2 cups almond flour
- 1/4 cup melted butter

- 2 tablespoons sugar-free sweetener (such as erythritol or stevia)
- 1/2 teaspoon vanilla extract

For the Filling:

- 8 ounces mascarpone cheese
- 1/2 cup heavy cream
- 1/4 cup sugar-free sweetener
- 1 teaspoon vanilla extract
- 1 teaspoon lemon zest

For the Topping:

- 1 cup fresh strawberries, hulled and sliced
- 1/2 cup fresh blueberries
- 1/2 cup fresh raspberries
- Fresh mint leaves for garnish (optional)

Directions:

1. Preheat your oven to 350°F (175°C). Grease a 9-inch tart pan with a removable bottom.
2. In a medium bowl, combine the almond flour, melted butter, sugar-free sweetener, and vanilla extract. Mix until the mixture is well combined and crumbly.
3. Press the crust mixture evenly into the bottom and up the sides of the prepared tart pan. Bake in the preheated oven for 10-12 minutes, or until the crust is golden brown. Remove from the oven and let cool completely.
4. In a large bowl, combine the mascarpone cheese, heavy cream, sugar-free sweetener, vanilla extract, and lemon zest. Beat with an electric mixer until the mixture is smooth and fluffy.
5. Spread the mascarpone filling evenly over the cooled crust.

6. Arrange the fresh strawberries, blueberries, and raspberries on top of the mascarpone filling in a decorative pattern.
7. Garnish with fresh mint leaves if desired.
8. Refrigerate the tart for at least 1 hour before serving to allow the filling to set.
9. Remove the tart from the pan and transfer to a serving plate. Slice and serve chilled.

Nutritional Values (per serving, based on 8 servings):

- Calories: 250
- Fat: 22g
- Carbohydrates: 8g
- Fiber: 3g
- Protein: 5g

Peanut Butter Cookies (Sugar-Free)

Ingredients:

- 1 cup natural peanut butter (no sugar added)
- 1/2 cup sugar-free sweetener (such as erythritol or stevia)
- 1 large egg
- 1 teaspoon vanilla extract
- 1/2 teaspoon baking soda
- 1/4 teaspoon salt

Directions:

1. Preheat your oven to 350°F (175°C). Line a baking sheet with parchment paper.
2. In a large bowl, combine the peanut butter, sugar-free sweetener, egg, vanilla extract, baking soda, and salt. Mix well until all ingredients are thoroughly combined.
3. Scoop tablespoon-sized portions of dough and roll them into balls. Place the

balls onto the prepared baking sheet, about 2 inches apart.

4. Using a fork, gently press down on each ball to create a crisscross pattern.

5. Bake in the preheated oven for 10-12 minutes, or until the edges are lightly browned. Be careful not to overbake.

6. Remove the cookies from the oven and let them cool on the baking sheet for 5 minutes before transferring them to a wire rack to cool completely.

Nutritional Values (per serving, based on 12 cookies):

- Calories: 130
- Fat: 10g
- Carbohydrates: 5g
- Fiber: 2g
- Protein: 5g

Lemon Ricotta Pie (Sugar-Free)

Ingredients:

For the Crust:

- 1 1/2 cups almond flour
- 1/4 cup melted butter
- 2 tablespoons sugar-free sweetener (such as erythritol or stevia)
- 1/2 teaspoon vanilla extract

For the Filling:

- 2 cups ricotta cheese
- 3 large eggs
- 1/2 cup sugar-free sweetener
- 1/4 cup fresh lemon juice
- 1 tablespoon lemon zest
- 1 teaspoon vanilla extract
- 1/4 teaspoon salt

Directions:

1. Preheat your oven to 350°F (175°C). Grease a 9-inch pie pan.

2. In a medium bowl, combine the almond flour, melted butter, sugar-free sweetener, and vanilla extract. Mix until the mixture is well combined and crumbly.

3. Press the crust mixture evenly into the bottom and up the sides of the prepared pie pan. Bake in the preheated oven for 10-12 minutes, or until the crust is golden brown. Remove from the oven and let cool slightly.

4. In a large bowl, combine the ricotta cheese, eggs, sugar-free sweetener, fresh lemon juice, lemon zest, vanilla extract, and salt. Beat with an electric mixer until the mixture is smooth and well combined.

5. Pour the filling into the pre-baked crust and spread it out evenly.

6. Bake in the preheated oven for 45-50 minutes, or until the filling is set and the top is lightly golden.

7. Remove the pie from the oven and let it cool to room temperature. Then refrigerate for at least 2 hours, or until fully chilled.

8. Before serving, garnish with additional lemon zest if desired.

Nutritional Values (per serving, based on 8 servings):

- Calories: 220
- Fat: 16g
- Carbohydrates: 7g
- Fiber: 2g
- Protein: 10g

Chocolate Avocado Mousse

Ingredients:

- 2 ripe avocados
- 1/4 cup unsweetened cocoa powder
- 1/4 cup sugar-free sweetener (such as erythritol or stevia)
- 1/4 cup unsweetened almond milk (or any milk of your choice)
- 1 teaspoon vanilla extract
- 1/4 teaspoon salt
- Fresh berries or mint leaves for garnish (optional)

Directions:

1. Cut the avocados in half, remove the pits, and scoop the flesh into a blender or food processor.
2. Add the unsweetened cocoa powder, sugar-free sweetener, unsweetened almond milk, vanilla extract, and salt to the blender.
3. Blend until the mixture is smooth and creamy, stopping to scrape down the sides as needed.
4. Taste the mousse and adjust the sweetness if necessary by adding a bit more sugar-free sweetener.
5. Spoon the mousse into serving bowls or glasses and refrigerate for at least 1 hour to allow the flavors to meld and the mousse to firm up.
6. Before serving, garnish with fresh berries or mint leaves if desired.

Nutritional Values (per serving, based on 4 servings):

- Calories: 180
- Fat: 15g
- Carbohydrates: 10g
- Fiber: 7g
- Protein: 3g

Vanilla Almond Ice Cream (Sugar-Free)

Ingredients:

- 2 cups heavy cream
- 1 cup unsweetened almond milk
- 1/2 cup sugar-free sweetener (such as erythritol or stevia)
- 1 tablespoon vanilla extract
- 1/4 teaspoon almond extract
- 1/2 cup chopped almonds (optional)

Directions:

1. In a medium bowl, combine the heavy cream, unsweetened almond milk, sugar-free sweetener, vanilla extract, and almond extract. Whisk until the sweetener is fully dissolved and the mixture is well combined.
2. Pour the mixture into an ice cream maker and churn according to the manufacturer's instructions, typically about 20-25 minutes, until the ice cream reaches a soft-serve consistency.
3. During the last 5 minutes of churning, add the chopped almonds if using.
4. Transfer the ice cream to an airtight container and freeze for at least 2 hours, or until firm.

5. Before serving, let the ice cream sit at room temperature for a few minutes to soften slightly for easier scooping.

Nutritional Values (per serving, based on 8 servings):

- Calories: 220
- Fat: 20g
- Carbohydrates: 4g
- Fiber: 1g
- Protein: 3g

PART IV
THE 30-DAY KICKSTART

Starting a new dietary journey can be both exciting and challenging, especially when it involves managing a condition like diabetes. This section provides you with a structured, easy-to-follow 30-day meal plan to jumpstart your path to healthier eating. Each day includes balanced, nutritious meals that are low in carbs and sugar, yet full of flavor and variety. Alongside the meal plan, you'll find practical tips for shopping, meal prepping, and maintaining your new dietary habits. By the end of these 30 days, you'll not only have developed a repertoire of delicious and healthy recipes but also cultivated habits that will support your long-term health and well-being. Let this plan guide you toward a more vibrant, energetic, and balanced life.

30 DAYS MEAL PLAN TABLE

Day	Breakfast	Lunch	Dinner	Snack
1	Greek Yogurt Parfait with Berries and Nuts	Grilled Chicken Caesar Salad	Baked Salmon with Asparagus and Lemon-Dill Sauce	Almonds and Chia Seed Pudding
2	Spinach and Feta Omelet	Turkey and Avocado Roll-Ups	Beef and Broccoli	Veggie Chips and Guacamole
3	Cinnamon Almond Flour Pancakes	Quinoa and Black Bean Salad	Grilled Steak with Garlic Butter	Mixed Nuts and Seeds
4	Chia Seed Pudding with Coconut Milk	Mediterranean Veggie Wrap (Low-Carb)	Herb-Crusted Pork Chops with Cauliflower Mash	Cheese and Fruit Platter
5	Low-Carb Blueberry Muffins	Broccoli and Cheddar Soup	Vegetarian Stuffed Zucchini Boats	Peanut Butter Celery Sticks
6	Smoked Salmon and Cream Cheese Bagel	Shrimp and Avocado Salad	Slow Cooker Pulled Pork	Kale Chips
7	Vegetable Hash with Eggs	Beef Lettuce Wraps	Low-Carb Shepherd's Pie	Spiced Pumpkin Seeds
8	Keto Breakfast Sandwich	Spinach and Goat Cheese Stuffed Portobello Mushrooms	Pan-Seared Tilapia with Lemon Butter Sauce	Hard-Boiled Eggs
9	Protein-Packed Smoothie Bowl	Tuna Salad Stuffed Tomatoes	Lamb Chops with Mint Pesto	Caprese Salad Skewers
10	Almond Butter and Banana Shake	Cauliflower Fried Rice	Seared Scallops with Cauliflower Puree	Greek Yogurt Dip with Veggies
11	Cottage Cheese with Pineapple	Zucchini Noodle Pad Thai	Chicken Parmesan	Almond and Chia Seed Pudding

			(Breaded with Almond Flour)
12	Baked Avocado Eggs	Chicken and Vegetable Soup	Beef Stir-Fry with Bell Peppers and Snow Peas	Veggie Chips and Guacamole
13	Zucchini Bread (Sugar-Free)	Egg Salad on Rye Bread (Low-Carb)	Grilled Salmon with Asparagus and Lemon-Dill Sauce	Mixed Nuts and Seeds
14	Turkey Sausage Breakfast Burrito (Low-Carb)	Portobello Mushroom Pizza	Vegetarian Stir Fry with Tofu	Cheese and Fruit Platter
15	Steel-Cut Oats with Apples	Balsamic Grilled Vegetables	Baked Garlic Parmesan Chicken	Peanut Butter Celery Sticks
16	Spinach and Mushroom Breakfast Casserole	Chicken Taco Salad	Vegan Chili	Kale Chips
17	Flaxseed and Walnut Porridge	Asian Chicken Lettuce Wraps	Slow Cooker Beef Stew	Spiced Pumpkin Seeds
18	Tomato and Basil Frittata	Cucumber and Hummus Sandwiches	Baked Trout with Lemon and Herbs	Hard-Boiled Eggs
19	Raspberry Almond Muffins	Lentil and Veggie Bowl	Garlic Shrimp with Spaghetti Squash	Caprese Salad Skewers
20	Coconut Yogurt and Mixed Berries	Keto Chicken Salad	Low-Carb Jambalaya	Greek Yogurt Dip with Veggies
21	Low-Carb Granola	Greek Yogurt Chicken Salad	Roast Turkey with Low-Carb Stuffing	Almond and Chia Seed Pudding
22	Pepper and Egg White Scramble	Stuffed Bell Peppers	Lemon Basil Chicken over Spinach	Veggie Chips and Guacamole

23	Protein Pancakes	Cobb Salad	Beef and Broccoli	Mixed Nuts and Seeds
24	Turkey Bacon and Avocado Wrap	Cream of Mushroom Soup	Herb-Crusted Pork Chops with Cauliflower Mash	Cheese and Fruit Platter
25	Greek Yogurt Parfait with Berries and Nuts	Grilled Chicken Caesar Salad	Baked Salmon with Asparagus and Lemon-Dill Sauce	Peanut Butter Celery Sticks
26	Spinach and Feta Omelet	Turkey and Avocado Roll-Ups	Beef and Broccoli	Kale Chips
27	Cinnamon Almond Flour Pancakes	Quinoa and Black Bean Salad	Grilled Steak with Garlic Butter	Spiced Pumpkin Seeds
28	Chia Seed Pudding with Coconut Milk	Mediterranean Veggie Wrap (Low-Carb)	Herb-Crusted Pork Chops with Cauliflower Mash	Hard-Boiled Eggs
29	Low-Carb Blueberry Muffins	Broccoli and Cheddar Soup	Vegetarian Stuffed Zucchini Boats	Caprese Salad Skewers
30	Smoked Salmon and Cream Cheese Bagel	Shrimp and Avocado Salad	Slow Cooker Pulled Pork	Greek Yogurt Dip with Veggies

CONCLUSION

Making significant changes to your diet and lifestyle can be a challenging journey, but it's also incredibly rewarding. By following the meal plans, recipes, and tips provided in this book, you have taken crucial steps toward better health and well-being.

Throughout these pages, we've explored a variety of delicious, low-carb, and low-sugar recipes designed to keep your blood sugar levels stable and your body nourished. From hearty breakfasts and satisfying lunches to flavorful dinners and tempting snacks, each meal is crafted to support your health goals without compromising on taste.

The 30-day kickstart plan has equipped you with a practical and structured approach to integrating these healthy habits into your daily routine. By now, you should feel more confident in your ability to plan and prepare meals that suit your dietary needs. Remember, the key to lasting change is consistency and making choices that you can sustain over the long term.

It's important to continue exploring and experimenting with new recipes and ingredients to keep your meals interesting and enjoyable. Involve your family and friends in your journey; having a support system can make a significant difference. Share your successes, challenges, and favorite recipes with them, fostering a community of shared goals and mutual encouragement.

Don't forget to listen to your body and adjust your meal plans as needed. Everyone's nutritional needs are different, and what works for one person may not work for another. Be patient with yourself and stay committed to your health journey, even if you encounter setbacks along the way.

As you continue on this path, keep educating yourself about diabetes management and healthy living. Stay updated on new research, try out new recipes, and keep an open mind to different approaches that might work for you. Your dedication to improving your health is commendable, and every small step you take brings you closer to a healthier, happier life.

Thank you for allowing this book to be a part of your journey. May you find joy, health, and fulfillment in every meal you prepare and every step you take toward better health?

SCAN THE QR CODE AND IMMEDIATELY ACCESS YOUR 3 SPECIAL BONUSES IN DIGITAL FORMAT!

Made in United States
Orlando, FL
06 October 2024

52401842R00065